EQUAL JUSTICE
The Courage of Ada Lois Sipuel

EQUAL JUSTICE
The Courage of Ada Lois Sipuel

WILLIAM BERNHARDT

Dedicated to all the future young rebels who, like Ada Sipuel, have the courage to oppose injustice.

No State shall make or enforce any law which shall abridge
the privileges or immunities of citizens of the United States;
nor shall any State deprive any person of life, liberty, or property,
without due process of law; nor deny to any person within its
jurisdiction the equal protection of the laws.

FOURTEENTH AMENDMENT TO THE
UNITED STATES CONSTITUTION

1

SMART MOUTH

"Ada Lois!"

Ten-year old Ada Sipuel jerked her head around. She knew that voice well. It belonged to her little sister, Helen. Helen was a shy girl, like Ada. She did not like to attract attention, especially when she was in the white part of town.

"Ada! Hurry!"

Ada dropped the grocery bag she was carrying and ran. She knew it had been a mistake to come here. Chickasha, Oklahoma was a wonderful, warm community—as long as she stayed near home. She always felt safe among friends, or family, or at her school. But her parents had warned her not to leave the black neighborhood.

Ada ran as fast as she could—and she could run plenty fast. Helen must have wandered off while Ada was looking at the school the white children attended. She had never seen anything like it before. It had big rooms and a fancy playground. The library was filled with books, and Ada loved books. She was distracted and forgot to watch Helen. Now her little sister might be in serious danger.

She heard her sister scream again. "Ada! Come quick!" Then she heard something else.

"What's the matter, little girl? Can't you read? Don't they teach you dumb coloreds to read?"

1

Ada rounded the end of the school building. She found her little sister lying in the dirt. A much older white girl was hovering over her. This girl's fists were pressed against her hips. She looked angry.

"Why, look what we got here," the angry girl said, when she saw Ada. "Another one. Are you as dumb as this girl?" Ada looked down at her sister. Helen was dirty and her right knee was scraped. She was crying. The white girl was wearing a nice skirt and a matching sweater. It was prettier than anything Ada had to wear, even on church days.

Ada was scared, but she had to help Helen. She walked right up to the white girl. She did not stop until they were only a foot apart. Ada knew she had to show the older, much larger girl that she was not afraid. Even though she was. "I'm not dumb," Ada said.

"You are. You're the dumbest looking colored I ever saw."

Ada knew it would be smarter to hold her tongue, but she could not help herself. She never could. That's why everyone in her family called her "smart mouth."

"You're the one who's dumb," Ada said. "If you weren't so dumb, you wouldn't think it's fun to pick on a little girl." Ada could see this made the other girl even madder than she was before.

"You must be dumb to get so lost."

"I'm not lost," Ada said.

"Then what're you doing here? This ain't colored town." She picked up a dirt clod and threw it at Ada.

Ada ducked. "I know that. We came here to get some sugar at the store."

"Then why were you at the school?"

That question was harder for Ada to answer. She was not entirely sure what to say. "Today's Saturday. There's no school. I've got as much right to be here as anyone."

"Is that what you think?" The other girl gave Ada a shove. "Just leave my sister and me alone."

"Or what? Are you going to fight me?"

Ada had been in fights before. Her older brother, Lemuel, had taught her how to handle herself. She knew how to block and throw punches. She could step back to avoid punches. She knew how to move in when she saw an opening. She had learned to deal with threats, dares, double-dares, and double-dog dares.

"I don't want to fight you," Ada said quietly. Then she added: "But I will if I have to."

"I'm not afraid of you," the other girl said. "I know who you are. You're that preacher's girl."

Ada stood her ground. "My father may be a preacher, but I'm not."

"I'll tell you what I think you are. I think you're an uppity little nigger." The girl shoved her backward and tripped her. Ada hit the ground hard. It knocked the breath out of her. She wasn't sure what to do. At school, the bullies she fought had all been her age, and they had all been boys. She had never known a girl to be a bully before. She did not like the idea of fighting another girl. She knew it could be dangerous to fight anyone, here in the white part of town. She also knew her father did not approve of fighting.

She remembered something her father had told her. "If something's worth having, it's worth fighting for." She also recalled his words on the day he sent her to school for the first time. "Always stand up for what's right."

"What's the matter?" The white girl said, hovering over Ada and Helen. "You coloreds too stupid to pick yourselves up out of the dirt?" And with that, she kicked Helen in the side.

Ada threw herself at the girl with all the strength she could muster. They both fell to the ground. They rolled back and forth in the dirt. First Ada was on top, then the other girl, then Ada again.

That was when Ada learned the main difference between fighting boys and fighting girls. Girls scratch.

Ada screamed. "How dare you!" She wondered if she would be scarred for life. Her face was bleeding.

The girl tried to hit her, but Ada blocked the punch. She pinned the girl's arms back and held her to the ground. The girl tried to scratch Ada again, but she could not get her arms free. Ada made a fist.

The other girl screamed. "Stop! Please stop!"

"Are you going to hurt my sister anymore?"

"No! Just leave." As Ada crawled off her, she added, "Go back where you belong, and teach your stupid sister to read."

"What makes you think my sister doesn't know how to read?" Ada asked, brushing the dirt off her dress.

The white girl pushed herself to her feet and pointed at a nearby sign.

Then Ada understood everything.

"You did."

"Did not."

"You will."

"I won't."

"It is."

"It isn't."

Ada sat in her father's lap. They were having their usual after-dinner conversation. She loved these times. Her father, Bishop Travis B. Sipuel, had taught her to be respectful to grownups. When they were alone, however, she was allowed to "smart mouth" as much as she pleased.

Ada and Helen had come home directly after the fight. Ada had not even stopped to pick up the sugar she dropped. There was no hiding what had happened. They looked like they had been in a fight.

Ada's mother bathed her and washed her hair and put it in three long braids. Then they had dinner. No one mentioned the fight. Now that she was in her father's lap, though, the time had come.

"You know that Jesus told us to turn the other cheek," her father said. "He didn't set with fighting."

"Do you think Jesus wanted me to let Helen get all beat up?" Ada shot back.

"Of course not. But could you have avoided the fight?" Ada's smart mouth stayed quiet a moment. She knew she probably could have avoided the fight, if she had ignored the mean girl and just taken Helen away with her. She was not going to admit that, though. "You always told me to stand up for what's right."

"And I meant it," her father said. "But it's possible to make a stand without swinging a fist. There are other ways to fight." He held her by the shoulders and gave her a hug. "You're a smart girl. You'll figure it out."

The next day, after church, Ada's mother took her back to downtown Chickasha. She wanted to see where all the commotion had happened.

"You know you had no business leaving our neighborhood," Ada's mother said. She held Ada's hand and kept her close to her side. "Especially not with your little sister."

"But you told me to get some sugar," Ada protested.

"At the corner store!"

"They were out of sugar. I didn't want to let you down."

"Is that so."

"Yes! I knew you needed sugar to make gingerbread."

"And you wanted your gingerbread dessert." Her mother nodded. "I think I understand now."

She walked quickly through the main street of town, keeping her eyes lowered, staying out of white people's way. "One thing I don't understand, though, Ada. What were you doing at that school?"

Ada hesitated. "I . . . don't know. I was just curious about it."

"And what did you see?"

"Oh, Mother—it was wonderful! The building was new and they had sidewalks. Real paved sidewalks! And a playground. And when I peeked through the window, I saw the classrooms. They were huge and clean and—they had so many books. You can't believe how many books there were." Like all smart girls, Ada loved to read. But sometimes she had a hard time getting books.

"Mother," Ada asked, "why doesn't our school look like their school?"

"It's the law," her mother explained. "Everything has to be segregated."

Ada had heard people try to explain this before. She knew that Chickasha—for that matter, all of Oklahoma—was segregated. That meant black people were kept separate from white people. It had always been that way. Chickasaw Indians originally settled the city. They brought their black slaves with them. After slavery ended, many other black people joined the black community already there. White people soon followed. Although the black people and the Indians had been there longer, the white people controlled the government. The government insisted on segregation. Ada had learned that segregation followed people through their entire lives. It started when they were born, in segregated hospitals. It continued when they were educated, in segregated schools. And it ended when they were buried, in segregated cemeteries.

Some people said that was the only way the two races could coexist. Ada's parents did not agree. "There's only one Constitution," her father often said. "Only one Bible. The law should be the same for everyone." But when Ada looked at the fancy new school the white children attended, she knew the law was not the same for everyone.

"Here we are," Ada's mother said, when they arrived at the school. "Now show me where the fight was."

Ada showed her. She could still see the scuffed footprints from the fight.

"And where is this sign that caused so much bother?"

Ada pointed. It was next to a water fountain just outside the front door to the school.

The Sign said: Whites Only.

Helen was not old enough to read the sign. She had started to drink from the fountain. That was why the white girl chased her and hit her.

"So that's it?" Ada's mother asked.

Ada was not sure if she was angry at her or something else.

"You fought over this sign?"

"Mother," Ada said, "this isn't right. It's not fair."

"Listen to me, Ada, and you listen well. How many sides does that sign have?"

Ada thought a moment before answering. Was this a trick question? "Two."

"That's right. And we both know what the front side says. What's on the other side?"

Ada checked, just to be sure. "Nothing."

"That's right. The other side doesn't say anything." She took her daughter's face into her hands and looked directly into her eyes. "You can write whatever you want on it."

2

TWO WORLDS

Ada sat on the back porch of her home. She was about to take a bite out of her favorite dessert—a warm slice of gingerbread. Ada knew that her family was lucky. Her father's job allowed them to have one of the nicer houses in the black part of Chickasha. There was a large wood-burning stove in the kitchen. They had another pot-bellied cast-iron stove in the living room. The backyard was large and included a chicken house, a smokehouse (which Ada and Helen often used as a playhouse), and a pigpen with two hogs in it. They had a backyard well and an outhouse. There was no indoor plumbing in this part of town.

"Ada, would you like to have all the gingerbread you want for the rest of your life?"

Ada stared at her big brother, Lemuel. "Of course I'd like that. But you know it's impossible."

"No. It's possible."

Ada's eyes narrowed. She did not see how that could be.

Lemuel knew a lot of things, though. He was in the sixth grade. "Okay, how?"

"Plant a gingerbread tree."

"A gingerbread tree! There's no such thing."

"Course there is. Where do you think gingerbread comes from?"

"From the kitchen. I've seen Mother make it."

"Yes, but where does she get the ingredients?"

"From the store."

"And where do they get them?"

Ada had to stop and think. She really did not know. "Are you saying they come from a tree?"

"Course they do. Where else would they come from? Get yourself a gingerbread tree and you'll have gingerbread for life."

Ada stared at the warm gingerbread she held in her hand. Gingerbread for life. Just the thought of it made her light-headed. "How do we get one?"

"It's easy," Lemuel shrugged. "If you know how." "Tell me!"

"Don't eat your piece. Take it over by the fence in a bright area that gets lots of sun and plant it."

Ada got a little shovel out of her mother's garden and did just as he told her to do.

"That's not enough," Lemuel warned. "Now you have to water it."

"Okay, I'll water it."

"With milk."

Ada poured her glass of buttermilk all over the freshly dug soil. She came back to the porch steps—and found her mother staring at her. When Ada told her what had happened, her mother was very upset.

"Lemuel," her mother said, "that was a very bad thing you did." Their mother, Martha Smith Sipuel, was a beautiful, tall, light-skinned woman—but she could look scary when she was angry. "I'm going to spank you."

Ada tried to understand. Did this mean there would be no gingerbread tree?

"You come, too, Ada," her mother said. "I'm spanking you next."

Ada pressed her hands against her chest. "Me? Why me?"

Her mother led her inside. "What have I always told you children?

What are the two things I cannot and will not abide? One is lying."

"I didn't lie!" Ada protested. "I didn't!"

"And the other is being simple. I'm going to punish you for being so foolish."

Inside, Ada's father heard all the ruckus. He came into the kitchen and asked what was happening. Ada's mother explained that she was going to spank Ada.

Hope sprang up in Ada's heart. She knew her father did not believe in spanking. He thought it was just another kind of hitting. Unfortunately, he had never stopped his wife from spanking the children when she thought they needed it. Ada ran to her father and wrapped herself around his legs, hoping for protection.

Her father frowned. "How many swats is she to get?"

Ada's mother thought for a moment. "Four."

"I'll take them for her."

Ada's eyes widened like balloons. She thought he must be joking. She watched as her father bent over—and his wife gave him four swats on the backside. She did not hold back, either.

Ada felt very bad. Even if she thought she had not done anything wrong, she should have taken her own punishment.

When the spanking was over, Ada's mother gave her father a stern look. "I'm not sure this is going to make that girl any smarter."

Her father gave Ada a long look. "I think it might."

Ada loved school. She loved all her subjects, but her favorites were history and reading. She never tired of reading. Her favorite author was Mark Twain. His stories always made her laugh. Sometimes they made her think, too. What could be funnier than Tom Canty pretending to be royal in *The Prince and the Pauper*? Or knights riding bicycles in *A Connecticut Yankee in King Arthur's Court*?

She loved her after-school activities, too. By the time Ada was fourteen, she was a soloist in the school choir, sang in the *a cappella* group, and was a guard on the girls' basketball team.

Ada was happy there, but she could not help remembering the white school on the other side of town. She remembered the big classrooms, the shiny lockers, the clean new desks, and all the books. And she remembered the playground. There were no playgrounds at Ada's school. In fact, there were no parks or playgrounds anywhere in Chickasha where black children were allowed to play.

Ada's father had tried to explain to her why the two schools were so different. Although the United States Constitution said that schools must be equal, the Oklahoma Constitution forbade mixing races in schools. The Oklahoma school system was financed by two separate tax rates. The tax money for white schools was far greater than the money for black schools. Chickasha had as many schools for white children as all of Grady County did for black students. Lincoln school, where Ada attended, took students of all ages, from first grade through twelfth grade.

Ada got along well with her principal, Mr. Parrish. Her smart mouth sometimes got her in trouble. But Mr. Parrish knew she was a good student and encouraged her to work hard.

One day, Mr. Parrish met Ada in the hallway. "Ada, may I talk with you for a moment?"

Ada wondered what was happening. Since when did the principal ask permission to talk to a student? "Sure."

"Do you like this school?" Mr. Parrish was a tall, large man. He towered over her. She could not see around him on either side.

Ada loved her school, but she was not about to tell him that. "It's all right, I guess."

Mr. Parrish grinned. "I like it, too. But I have a problem. A lot of things in this school aren't the way they should be. I do my best, but there isn't enough money to make this school right. I take hand-me-down desks and chalkboards and anything else I can get from the white schools in town. But it still isn't enough."

So that was why the equipment at Lincoln did not compare with the equipment at the white school. They were using the other schools' leftovers.

"Here's my problem, Ada. The school board is coming for their annual visit. They call it a visit, but it's more like an inspection. They bring their wives, look the place over, and decide whether it should be funded for another year."

Ada was confused. "So what's the problem?"

"I'm afraid all those big shot men and their wives won't like what they see here. And they'll shut the school down." "Maybe that would be good," Ada said. "Then we could all go to the nice new school across town."

"Who are you kidding, Ada Lois Sipuel? They'll never let black children attend that school. It's against the law. If we lose Lincoln— we'll be left with nothing."

Ada felt a cold chill race up her spine. No school? No learning? No books? She could not stand to think about it. "But—they have to give us some kind of school. Don't they?"

"I hear they're talking about closing this school and saying you can go to school in Oklahoma City."

"Oklahoma City!" Oklahoma City was a long way from Chickasha. The black school there was far worse and more crowded than Lincoln. "They know we can't go there. We'd be left with no school at all."

Mr. Parrish folded his hands. "Now I think you understand the problem."

It wasn't right. It wasn't fair.

Ada remembered her father's words. If something's worth having, it's worth fighting for.

"All right," she told her principal. "What can I do to help?"

M r. Parrish chose Ada because he knew she was a fighter—and a leader. She got all of her friends to help get the school in shape. She got some of the teachers to help, too. They put red oil on the old wooden floor to give it some luster. They washed the windows. Some of them were broken, but Ada managed to get local merchants to contribute glass for new windows. The chalkboards got a thorough scrubbing and painting. The students even cleaned the erasers by beating them against rocks. There was so much chalk dust in the air that some people passing by thought the school was on fire.

As scheduled, the members of the school board—all of them white—arrived with their wives. Ada and her friends converted the home economics classroom into a banquet hall. They put borrowed lace tablecloths over the workstations to make them look like dining tables. They borrowed silver and everything else they would need to put on a fine meal. Ada persuaded the best cook in the neighborhood to prepare a fried chicken feast.

While the meal was served, Ada and her friends stayed outside. They kept the halls clear and the other classrooms quiet. The school board members ate and ate and ate. After this huge and wonderful meal, they were so sleepy they barely looked at the rest of the school. They poked their heads into a few classrooms, nodded, and left. Not one of them expressed the slightest hint that they saw anything they did not like.

The next day, Mr. Parrish stopped Ada in the hall. He was beaming.

"Ada! Great news! The school board gave us an excellent report."

Ada was pleased the efforts she and her friends had made were not wasted. "I'm glad."

"We can all relax. There's no chance they'll try to close the school now."

"Since they liked the school so much, is there any chance they might give us some more money?"

Mr. Parrish frowned. "Any chance of more books? A playground? A science lab?" Mr. Parrish shook his head.

"We got a glowing report! Why should we get half as much money as the white schools? Why do we have to use their hand-me-downs?"

Mr. Parrish shrugged. "That's the way it is, Ada. That's the way it's always been for segregated schools. Separate but equal."

"They got the separate part right. They need to work on the equal."

"Some things you just have to accept, Ada."

I do not, Ada thought, as she walked away, angry and disappointed. After all that work, she had not made anything better. She had just made it possible for the school board to go on treating her school as it had always done.

That's the way it is, Mr. Parrish had said, and maybe he was right. But it did not have to be that way. And someday, Ada was determined that it would be different.

3

THE TURNING POINT

Ada had a lot of fun when she was in high school. Her favorite hangout, other than church and school, was John's Café. The café was only a block from Lincoln. Everyone passed it on the way to and from school. They could get big greasy hamburgers for fifteen cents. For a nickel they could listen to songs on the jukebox, including the jumping jive music that was sweeping the country.

Some of Ada's friends liked to dance to the music. John's old wooden floor would shimmy and shake under the weight of all those feet. One afternoon, the dancing was so strong the floor caved in beneath them! After it was fixed, everyone took it a little easier on the dance floor.

Two of the regulars at John's were Ada's brother Lemuel and his best friend, Warren Fisher. Warren was the son of the local Baptist preacher. He was a handsome boy, tall and slender, with gray eyes. Ada's parents liked Warren. He ran errands for Ada's mother. He helped her father around the house. He spent so much time at their home that they all treated him like a member of the family. Ada came to think of him as another brother.

Ada's favorite activity in high school was playing basketball. By the tenth grade, she was five feet, eight inches tall, which made her taller than most of the girls in her school. She was a guard. It was her job to make sure the players on the other team did not score. Ada was good at it. She never backed away from a scrap. She was so good, in fact, that her coach started asking members of the boys' team to play against her during practice. She did not want to risk the other members of the girls' team getting injured!

Ada's coach, Mrs. Bertha Fletcher, was strict and worked the team hard. She expected her team to observe not only the rules but also the spirit of the game. "It's not about whether you win or lose," she would tell her team. "It's how you play the game." She insisted on sportsmanlike conduct at all times. Although Ada and her teammates were talented, they were losing most of their games. Ada became discouraged. She could see the other teams were playing "dirty tricks," and not getting caught. That gave them a huge advantage.

Ada had no desire to be unsportsmanlike—but she did not much like losing, either. She talked to her coach about it.

"We could win some of these games, Coach," Ada insisted one day after practice. "I know we could. We just have to . . . play a little differently."

"It's not about winning." Mrs. Fletcher was a sizable woman, not one who encouraged argument from her players. "If you don't have your integrity, you don't have nothin'."

"I know that," Ada insisted. She muttered under her breath: "But I'd still rather win."

"Listen to me," Mrs. Fletcher said. "Where would this world be if everyone went around breaking the rules?"

Ada thought of all the ways she had seen the government twist, bend, and avoid the "separate but equal" rule, without ever quite breaking it. "I wouldn't break the rules. That would be wrong. But some of those girls out there can do some tricky moves so they don't quite break the rules. Again she spoke under her breath: "or at any rate, they don't get caught."

Mrs. Fletcher looked at her firmly. "You listen to me, Ada Lois Sipuel. I don't coach that kind of team. Do you understand me?"

Ada looked down at her sneakers. "Yes, Coach."

"My team plays a clean game. Always has and always will. Are we clear on that?"

"Yes, ma'am." Ada meant it, too. But she still didn't like losing.

Ada knew that some of the girls on other teams fouled players when they were about to score. Ada thought she could do that, too. The challenge was trying to do it without being caught. If the referee caught her, the other team would get a free shot—maybe two. And if she were caught by Coach Fletcher—that would be even worse.

Ada learned how to foul when a player on the other team was about to shoot—without being noticed. Or if she were noticed, she made it look like a big accident.

"Oops! I tripped!"

"Sorry about that. My shoestring came unlaced." "You came out of nowhere!"

"I was standing still. She ran into my elbow!"

As the basketball season went on, Ada got better and better at her "creative guarding." Several times after she pulled off a successful trick, she noticed Coach Fletcher on the sidelines. She was looking at Ada with narrowed eyes and a suspicious expression.

The most important thing Ada noticed, however, was that as she got better and better at creative guarding—her team started winning.

Eventually, Ada's team made it to the final game of the season. This game would decide whether they had a winning season. They were playing against their arch rivals. The gymnasium was packed. Almost everyone in the black community of Chickasha was there.

Before each game began, the team always sat on the locker room floor and listened to Coach Fletcher's advice. This time, however, the pre-game talk went on particularly long. The coach knew how many people had come to watch the game. She knew how important it was to some of the spectators.

"You are a fine team," Coach Fletcher told them. "You have come a long way this year. You have proven that you can be champions."

The entire team whooped and hollered.

"Don't forget everything you've learned this year. Don't forget the skills you've been practicing."

Ada's teammates assured the coach that they would not. "Most importantly, don't forget that you are all good players. You are trained athletes. Play hard"—she held up a finger—"but play fair. Remember—if you don't have your integrity, you don't have nothin."

The team jumped to their feet, cheering. *"All right! Yeah, We're ready! Bring 'em on! Let's go get 'em!"*

As they walked onto the court, Coach Fletcher took Ada aside. She looked directly into Ada's eyes and said: "Don't get caught, Sipuel. Just don't get caught."

Ada's mother was active in the NAACP—the National Association for the Advancement of Colored People. The NAACP fought to make sure that all people were treated fair and equally by the law. They had attorneys who filed suits in court whenever the law was broken or the "separate but equal" rule was not observed. Ada's mother worked with the local Chickasha chapter of the NAACP. She made sure everyone in the family read the NAACP magazine, The Crisis, which was edited by the famous civil rights activist, W. E. B. Dubois.

Ada's mother also made sure her family knew they were fighting for more than just schools and jobs. She told them about Henry

Argo, the last black man to be lynched in Oklahoma—right there in Chickasha. A few years before, Carl Dudley had been shot more than fifty times by an angry white gang. Bennie Simmons had been dragged from jail by a mob of more than a thousand men and hung. His body was left hanging for days over the Washita River about eighteen miles from Chickasha.

She told them why her father's family moved from Tulsa to Chickasha. Tulsa once had a thriving black community and prosperous business district known as the Black Wall Street. That ended in 1921, when the community was destroyed by a race riot in which hundreds of people died. When Ada was five years old, many people thought a race riot would break out in Chickasha. She remembered her father sitting by the door with an old musket all night long. He was a man of peace, but he still had to protect his family.

"Why do white people hate us so much?" Ada asked her mother one evening while she was getting ready for a NAACP meeting.

"They don't," her mother assured her. "Least not all of them. Not even most of them, I think."

"But some?" Ada asked.

Her mother sighed heavily. "Yes, some. But there are bad seeds everywhere you go. In every job, every race, every religion. You can't judge a group by their worst members. Lots of white people have performed wonderful, generous acts. Many white folk are working hard to make the world a better place for black Americans."

Ada's mother thought for a moment. "Honey, would you like to come to the meeting tonight? It's a very special meeting. I think you might like it."

Ada was excited at the thought of going to a grownup meeting. "Why is tonight special?"

"Because of the speaker," her mother said, as she adjusted her hat in the mirror. "He's a lawyer."

"What's so special about a lawyer?"

Her mother gave Ada a long look. "How many black lawyers have you met, young lady?"

Ada thought for a moment. Actually, she could only think of one.

"This man is special," her mother explained. "He went to school at Howard University, then practiced at a big law firm in New York. Now he's the chief counsel for the NAACP. He travels all around the country helping people. He's a very special man. You just come and see."

Ada went to the meeting. It was held at a local church. That was the biggest meeting place in the black part of the city. She was impressed by how many people were there, including people she knew were not NAACP members. Even many white people were present.

Her mother had been right. The speaker was a very special man. He was handsome, well groomed, well spoken, and smart. He had a big smile that lit up the room. He spent the first few minutes of his speech just telling funny stories. By the time he was ready to get serious, he already had the crowd on his side.

His name was Thurgood Marshall.

"We have reached a turning point in the history of our race. The thirteenth, fourteenth, and fifteenth amendments to the United States Constitution were passed almost one hundred years ago. Those laws were passed to ensure that everyone—everyone—is treated equally under the law." He paused. His voice suddenly became quiet. "It is time we enforced those laws."

Ada felt shivers rushing up and down her. She had never heard such a good speaker. His words, his tone of his voice, his facial expressions, and his gestures all helped make his points. He was extremely convincing.

"'Separate but equal' cannot and will not stand," Thurgood Marshall continued. "It is an affront to the letter and spirit of the US Constitution. We are taxed like other Americans. We are drafted like other Americans. Why are we not treated like other Americans? Why is this tolerated?"

Marshall slowly scanned the audience. "I will tell you, my friends. It is tolerated because it has become acceptable. But that puts us on a slippery slope. One inequity leads to another, then another. It doesn't have to be that way. Black Americans fought for their freedom from slavery. We fought poll taxes. We fought zoning laws that tried to tell us where we could and could not live. And now we must fight 'separate but equal.' Because that horrible phrase is a lie. Separate is not ever and never can be equal."

The crowd murmured and cheered. They greeted his words with thunderous applause.

"We need more people who are unwilling to accept things as they are. We need brave, courageous citizens who will stand up for what they believe in. We need people who understand the law well and can use it to our advantage. We need men and women who are not afraid to look inequality in the eye and say, no, sir! I will not abide you. I will not sit quietly while you twist the meaning of the law. A new day is dawning. And the name of that day is not separation, but equality!"

The crowd cheered. As Ada looked around the church, she saw that many of the people in the audience had tears in their eyes.

One of them was her mother.

While they were walking home, Ada made a promise to herself. "I'm not going to be one of those people who just accept things the way they are. I won't accept anything that keeps people separate and unequal. When I get older, I'm going to be a lawyer, just like Mr. Marshall. Then I'll try to make things better. For everyone."

4

HIGHER EDUCATION

Ada's parent did not let her date before high school. They would not even let her go out with friends on school nights. The one exception to this rule, Ada noticed, occurred whenever Warren was around. If he said he was going to the movies, Ada's mother would always let her go with him. In fact, sometimes she suggested it.

One night, Ada's mother suggested that Warren go with her to one of her school dances, as her chaperon. He danced with her several times. Ada assumed he was just being nice. Once, though, while they were waltzing, she turned her head suddenly and his lips brushed against her face. Ada assumed it had just been an accident. After all, Warren was practically her brother!

When Ada turned sixteen, her parents decided she was old enough to date. Her father gave her many stern talks about proper behavior. Her mother gave her many warnings. "You have to take care of yourself," she told Ada. "Protect your reputation. If you don't have your reputation, you don't have nothin.'"

"I thought that was integrity," Ida said. "If you don't have your integrity, you don't have nothin.'"

"That, too," her mother sniffed.

Ada's first real boyfriend was a classmate named Jesse Draper. She was allowed to go out with him on the weekends, although they were never supposed to be alone together. Ada's brother Lemuel usually kept a close eye on her. Ada thought that was very unfair.

Ada became friends with a girl Warren dated named Vivian. One weekend, Vivian told Ada that her mother would be out of town all weekend. Would Ada like to bring Jesse over to their place?

"Of course I would," Ada said. She had a hunch her parents might not approve. So she did not mention it to them.

Ada and Jesse came over to Vivian's house that night. Vivian chatted with them for a little while. Then she told them she needed to go to a party. She said she would be back in a few hours. They could stay if they wanted and make themselves at home.

They did. Jesse turned the lights down low. Then he put on some music and they danced together. They danced very slow and close, their bodies swaying together. Ada was just beginning to wonder what might happen next when all at once—the lights came on.

Warren was standing in the doorway. His eyes were the coldest shade of gray Ada had ever seen.

"We weren't doing anything," Ada explained hastily. "Vivian said it was okay for us to be here."

"I'll deal with Vivian later," Warren said, his voice very low. "I'm driving you home to your parents."

Jesse skedaddled just as quickly as his feet would carry him. By the time Ada was in Warren's car, she was crying. She knew Warren would tell her parents that she had been alone with a boy. She would be in big trouble. If she had almost gotten spanked for believing in gingerbread trees, imagine what she would get for this! Worst of all, she knew they would be disappointed in her. She couldn't bear thinking about that.

"Warren," she finally managed to say, "are you going to tell my parents?"

"I don't have any choice, Ada." His hands gripped the steering wheel so tightly his knuckles were white. "You did wrong. You know you did."

"But—do you have to tell them?"

"Your parents have always been good to me. I can't keep secrets from them. Especially not a secret like this."

They continued to drive in silence—except for the sound of Ada's sobbing. She cried all the way home. She knew that after this, her parents would never let her date again. They might not even let her go away to college next year. Her life would be ruined.

Finally, Warren pulled up in front of Ada's house. He turned off the engine, took a deep breath, then looked at Ada's tear-stained face.

"Ada," he said, "do you promise there was nothing going on?" Ada was so upset she could barely speak. "Y-yes."

"Have you ever done anything like this before?" "N-no," she choked.

"Are you ever going to do anything like this again?"

"No. Never."

Warren drew in his breath then slowly released it. "Well, then, I guess maybe I don't have to tell your parents this time."

Ada's eyes widened.

"But if I ever find out you've done anything like this again, I'll tell your mother and father. I'll tell them about this time, too. Understand?"

"I understand. Thank you, Warren!" Without even thinking, she threw her arms around him. When she realized what she had done, she expected him to push her away. But he never did.

Ada attended Langston University, Oklahoma's only black college, not far from Guthrie, Oklahoma. The college was perched on a high mound of red clay that the students called "the Hill." Langston was supported by the state. As usual, though, the facilities were not equal to those at white colleges. Oklahoma's tax laws, which applied a different tax base to black institutions, gave much less money to black schools. The buildings and dormitories were old and badly in need of repair. The library was out-of-date. The auditorium was in such bad shape it could barely be used. Worst of all, there were almost no sidewalks.

"Be sure to wear your old shoes when it rains," one of the older students warned Ada on her first day.

"Why is that?" Ada asked.

"Rain makes the Hill's red clay turn into mud," the student explained. "The mud gets so sticky and thick it's like cement. You step into that—it'll suck your shoes right off your feet! Even if you manage to get inside, the mud from everyone's shoes comes off on the floors and the carpets. It makes a tremendous mess. It's like having red paint all over everything!"

Ada made a point of wearing her oldest shoes anytime there was a hint of a rain.

Ada loved college. She loved learning new subjects. She loved being with other students who were smart, curious, and eager to talk over new ideas. Most of all, she loved the library. Even though many of the books were out-of-date and the roof leaked, Ada found lots of wonderful books she had never read before. They had a complete collection of Mark Twain books, including some she had never known existed. She spent a good deal of her spare time reading in the library.

Visiting the library was the best part of being in college. Going to the dining hall was the worst. That was not because Ada did not like food. The price for getting food was passing by the white woman at the front door who punched the students' meal tickets. She was mean, rude, and vulgar. If students were so much as a minute late, she would refuse to let them eat. Even when students were on time, she hurled abuse at them. She called them stupid, ugly, and ignorant. She also used unkind racial slurs. If a student objected to this treatment, she would turn them away without dinner. Ada first encountered this mean woman in 1944. The United States was at war with Germany. Some of the students compared the cafeteria woman to Gestapo soldiers they had seen in newsreels. They called her "Frau Cafeteria Lady."

Ada wondered how such a mean-spirited bigoted person could get a job at Langston University. What she learned was that state jobs— even those at Langston—were controlled by politicians. Local state senators could give jobs to their friends and supporters. Once they had the job, no one could fire them except the senator who had given them the job—not even the president of the university.

One evening, Ada saw the cafeteria lady be so rude that a friend of hers started to cry. Ada marched up to the woman. She did not care if she lost her dinner. She was going to tell this horrible person what she thought.

"If you can't do this job without being mean," Ada said, "you shouldn't have the job at all."

Frau Cafeteria Lady sneered at her with contempt. "White folks hired me. You niggers can't fire me."

Ada knew she couldn't fire the woman in the dining hall, but that did not mean she could not do anything about it. She remembered Thurgood Marshall's speech. He urged people to use civil disobedience—nonviolent protests against inequity. She remembered her own father's words: "If something's worth having, it's worth fighting for."

Ada organized a student boycott of the dining hall. She wrote a letter demanding that Frau Cafeteria Lady be removed. When she was not fired, the students took action. Under Ada's direction, they pooled their money to buy huge jars of peanut butter and jelly, long sausage rolls, and lots of bread. They bought enough food so that no one would have to go to the dining hall. Committees were formed to assemble the sandwiches. Floor captains in each dorm distributed them. Out of six hundred students, only ten showed up for dinner that night. The cafeteria staff was forced to throw away huge quantities of food.

At first, nothing happened. The cafeteria staff was certain the students would eventually get hungry. But the boycott continued. On the fourth day, the president of the university called Ada and some of the other students into his office to hear their complaints. Frau Cafeteria Lady was also present. "She is abusing her position," Ada said. "We should not have to endure this abuse just to get a meal."

Frau Cafeteria Lady denied that she had ever done anything wrong. She claimed that a few troublemakers who had grudges against her had trumped up the boycott. Eventually, they reached a compromise. An upper-class student worker began punching the tickets. Frau Cafeteria Lady remained in the dining hall, but she no longer had contact with the students and she kept her mouth shut.

Of course, Ada noted, she still kept her job.

One night while Ada was at home visiting her parents, she went to a friend's house. They talked late into the night— too late. Ada realized she should not walk home alone. She called her mother to ask someone to pick her up. Lemuel was out on a date, but Warren was there. He had joined the army about the time Ada went to college, but he was home on a temporary leave. Ada's mother said she would send Warren to walk Ada home.

It was a beautiful evening. The weather was cool and the stars were bright. Ada and Warren talked about many things and laughed a lot. Warren bought sodas and they talked about their plans for the future.

About a block from home, Warren stopped and, without any warning at all, put his arms around Ada and kissed her. Ada did not know what to think! She was surprised, shocked, angry—and maybe a little scared.

"Warren! What do you think you are doing?"

"Something I've been wanting to do for a long time."

"Well, you shouldn't have done it. You had no business doing it."

Warren didn't say anything.

"I'm going to tell my parents what you did," Ada said, marching ahead of him. "I'm going to tell them just as soon as I get home."

"No, you're not," Warren said, jumping in front of her. "I'm going to tell them myself."

The conversation in Ada's living room that night was tense. Both her mother and father listened as she and Warren explained what had happened. Warren did not deny what he had done. Ada expected her parents to be outraged, but their reaction was quieter. Several times she saw the two of them exchanging looks. She did not know what that meant.

Ada's father steepled his fingers, which Ada always thought made him look as if he were praying. "What do you have to say for yourself, Warren?"

Warren stood up straight. "Bishop Sipuel, I'd like to request your permission to court your daughter."

There was a long silence.

"Well," Ada's mother finally replied, pointing a finger in Warren's direction, "Ada is right. You had no business kissing her without asking her permission."

Warren lowered his head. "Yes, ma'am."

"However," Ada's father added, clearing his throat, "you have our permission to seek our daughter's hand."

Warren's eyes brightened. "I do?"

Ada's father nodded. "Heaven knows you've got your work cut out for you," he said, glancing at Ada out the corner of his eye. "But if you think you're up to the challenge, then by all means, you have our blessing."

"That goes for you, too, Mrs. Sipuel?"

"That goes for me, too, Warren. But for heaven's sake, next time you want to kiss a girl, give her some warning."

Ada was outraged. Why was he not being punished for the awful thing he had done? Why didn't anyone ask *her* if she wanted Warren to "seek her hand?" She stomped to her room and slammed the door behind her, furious.

Within six months, Ada was totally, madly, and permanently in love with Warren. A few weeks later, they were married.

5

STUDENT SMART MOUTH

Ada and Warren were wed in the living room of her parents' home. They did not have a honeymoon. They had no time or money to go away, and no hotel in town accepted black guests. So they spent their wedding night in Ada's parents' home.

The next day, Ada went back to school at Langston, and Warren returned to Fort Sill, in Lawton, Oklahoma, where he was a member of a first-rate—but segregated—field artillery unit. A few days later, he was sent to the European battlegrounds of World War II.

Ada's junior year in college was unusually rainy—and at Langston, unbearably muddy. Some students lost all the shoes they had. Others carried their shoes to class, washing off their feet in the bathroom before putting them on. Ada thought this had gone long enough.

With a group of concerned students, Ada formed a committee to improve conditions at Langston. They first talked to the leader of the university, President Harrison. After a long conversation, though, Ada realized there was nothing he could do. The state senate had not allocated enough money to Langston to make the needed repairs and improvements. With the war going on, it was very difficult to obtain private donations.

The students left the meeting disappointed.

"That's it, then," said Thelma, one of Ada's best friends. "There's nothing more we can do."

Ada was not willing to give up so easily. "I don't know about that."

"You heard what he said," Thelma insisted. "He doesn't control the flow of money."

"Then we should talk to someone who does," Ada replied.

Thelma stared at her. "You're talking about the state senate."

"I know that. Let's contact Senator Ritzhaupt. He should take care of the problems in his district."

"Maybe the white problems," one of the other students said. "But he's not going to help us. That's why the school is in the shape it's in."

Ada gave him a stern look. "Don't be one of those people who just accept things the way they are. Anything worth having is worth fighting for."

"So what are we going to do?" Thelma asked.

"We're going to get an appointment to meet our senator."

"How? We can't even afford a long distance phone call."

"Maybe not," Ada said. "But I noticed when we were in President Harrison's office that he had a phone . . ."

That afternoon, while the president and his secretary were away, Ada and her friends slipped into his office and placed a call to Senator Ritzhaupt. They were surprised when he answered his own phone.

"This is Senator Ritzhaupt. What can I do for you?"

Ada felt a catch in her throat. She was talking to a state senator!

"Sir," she said slowly, catching her breath, "I represent a group of students at Langston University."

"That's just fine," the senator said. "Langston is in my district. What can I do for you?"

"Sir ... do you have any idea what the conditions are like here?" Ritzhaupt cleared his throat. "Well, it's been a while since I was out there ..."

"It's bad, senator. The buildings need fixing. We need books and equipment. And the grounds are so muddy you can't walk to class without losing a shoe!"

The senator chuckled. "Well, these are hard times."

"I know, sir. But I also know the other colleges in the state are getting money. Why aren't we?"

"That's a complicated question. What is it you'd like me to do?"

"We'd like to come visit you at the Capitol building to discuss all the improvements that need to be made."

"I'll do you one better, young lady. I'll come out to campus tomorrow myself and meet with you. You can show me what it is you think needs to be done."

Ada was surprised—but pleasantly surprised. When she hung up the phone, she closed her eyes and prayed.

"Dear God, please let it rain tomorrow. We need lots of rain when the good senator arrives."

When President Harrison learned that Ada and her friends had contacted Senator Ritzhaupt without telling him, he was upset. He called the students into his office and told them that it was inappropriate for them to contact the senator directly.

Ada closed her eyes and thought quietly, *I'm glad he doesn't know we used his phone to do it!*

President Harrison allowed the meeting to take place, but he cautioned the students that they were to be calm and polite at all times. They could tell the senator their ideas, but they were not to criticize the university. After all, the state might decide to punish troublemakers by cutting the college's funding even further. It was even possible that they might close the university altogether, forcing black students to go to college out of state.

"The senator is our friend," President Harrison said sternly. "And we want him to remain our friend. Don't upset him."

"We have to tell him what we think," Ada insisted. "But we'll do our best not to cause any problems."

"You'd better," President Harrison said sharply. "If I learn that any student has undercut my authority, I will exact the most stern punishments available to me."

Ada knew what he was saying. She could be thrown out of school. Then she would be forced to go to college out of state—which she could not afford.

"I won't embarrass you, sir," Ada said, as she left the president's office. But she still prayed for rain.

The rain did not arrive, but Senator Ritzhaupt did. Ada and her friends were careful to remain calm and polite at all times. But they still told him everything that needed to be done at the university.

Senator Ritzhaupt was also calm and polite. Ada was impressed that he had taken time on such short notice to come to Langston. But he did not offer any help. He admitted that there was room for improvement. He insisted, however, that the facilities were adequate.

"They may be adequate," Ada said, "but they are nowhere near the equal of the white colleges in Oklahoma."

The senator smiled. "Those colleges are funded by a different tax base."

"Aren't all schools supposed to be equal?" Ada asked. She was not going to let him get away with an easy answer. "Don't ask for too much," Senator Ritzhaupt said, as he prepared to leave. "You're lucky you people have any college at all."

Ada watched as he drove away, disappointed and unhappy. If only it had rained! In her heart, though, she knew that it would make no difference. As long as the state could get away with separate and unequal, it would.

Someday, Langston will be equal to the other colleges in this state, she told herself. It was important for everyone to have a chance at a first-rate education. She would not give up this fight.

When Warren was on leave from the army, he was able to return to America. He spent every second he could with his newlywed wife. On a few occasions, Warren slipped away from his official duties so he could spend a little extra time with his sweetheart. He always managed to return to the base before his absence was noticed.

Finally, the time came when he had to ship back overseas. Ada and Warren walked together to the bus stop. Ada told him about her problems at the university.

"I don't know what more I can do," she said. "I've gone to President Harrison, and I've gone to Senator Ritzhaupt. What else is there?"

Warren thought for a moment. "What about that man who used to come to your house? You know, when your mother hosted her NAACP meetings? The writer."

Ada knew who he was thinking about. Roscoe Dunjee, the editor of *The Black Dispatch*, an outstanding paper published in Oklahoma City.

She had never considered going to the press with these problems. She wondered if there was anything he could do. The time came when Ada and Warren had to say goodbye. They kissed many times and hugged each other tightly. Ada was worried. The fighting had gotten much worse in Europe since D-Day. Too many American soldiers were being killed. "Don't worry about me," Warren said. "Nothing's going to happen. I'll be back."

Warren started to get on the bus, then turned and kissed her again. The bus driver felt so sorry for them that he held the bus as long as he could. Warren dried her eyes and they kissed one last time—while a bus full of strangers watched. Then the bus pulled away and Ada returned to Langston.

As soon as possible, Ada arranged a meeting with Roscoe Dunjee. He had been a member of Langston's very first graduating class. He was naturally concerned about the poor conditions at the school. Since graduating, he had become one of the most important black Americans in Oklahoma. His weekly editorials reminded her of Thurgood Marshall's speech. She was not surprised to learn that Dunjee and Marshall had worked together at the NAACP.

Dunjee had been involved in several important lawsuits that changed the treatment of black people in Oklahoma. He had successfully opposed zoning laws that segregated housing in Oklahoma City. Another case that went all the way to the United States Supreme Court guaranteed blacks the right to a jury of their peers—not a jury that eliminated all blacks. Another Supreme Court case Dunjee financed eliminated Oklahoma laws that tried to prevent blacks from exercising their right to vote.

Ada talked with Dunjee for hours. He promised her that he would write about Langston University in his newspaper. Eventually, he said, if they could attract enough attention to the problems, something would be done. Although Ada had hoped for a more immediate solution, it was encouraging. "Let me ask you a question, Ada?" Dunjee asked. "What brought you to me?"

She did not want to admit the idea came from her husband. "I've seen you at my mother's house. She's always spoken highly of you."

"Your mother is a wonderful woman," Dunjee said enthusiastically. "A tireless worker. Full of spirit and drive." A small smile crept across his face. "I think perhaps you have some of that in you, too, Ada."

Ada was suddenly embarrassed. She did not know what to say.

"Your mother's spirit and your father's sense of right and wrong," Dunjee said. "That's a good combination. A powerful combination." He tapped a finger against his lips. "A woman like you could make a difference in this world, Ada." Ada was confused. "I don't know what you mean."

He stood and showed her to the door. "Doesn't matter. You go on fighting your fights. There might come a time when all that spirit of yours might be useful. For something even more important than getting Langston out of the mud." Ada left the meeting both optimistic and confused. His final remarks had puzzled her. She did not know what to make of them.

What Ada could not possibly know was that her meeting with Roscoe Dunjee would change her life forever.

6

THE ROAD TO EQUAL

After Ada received her undergraduate degree, she wanted to go to law school. She remembered how Thurgood Marshall had spoken of the need for lawyers willing to fight for equal rights. Unfortunately, there was only one law school in the state of Oklahoma, at the University of Oklahoma in Norman. The OU law school, however, would not admit black students.

Ada's mother asked her to attend a meeting in her home. Ada was not surprised when she saw Dr. W. A. J. Bullock at the meeting. She had known him all her life. He had founded the local chapter of the NAACP. He directed it for twenty-five years. He was generally considered the chief spokesperson for Chickasha's black community.

Mr. Dunjee was also at the meeting. *They must be preparing to discuss something important,* Ada thought, *if both of them are here.*

Dr. Bullock was the first to speak to her. "Ada, I understand you want to attend law school."

"That's right," Ada said. "I'd like to use the law to make this a better world."

All the adults in the room looked at one another meaningfully.

"That's a very noble goal, Ada. Where were you thinking you might go to school?"

"I've considered Howard University in Washington, D.C., or Northwestern in Evanston, Illinois. But I can't afford to go out of state, at least not now."

"Ever thought about going to law school in Oklahoma?"

Ada stared at him. What could he be thinking? Surely he realized that OU did not accept black students. "I—I didn't think that was possible. OU is just for white students."

"And does that seem right to you?"

"Of course not. How can they claim the educational system is separate but equal when there's a state law school for white students but nothing for blacks?"

Bullock nodded. "Exactly."

Mr. Dunjee jumped in. "Ada, at the state NAACP convention last year, we devised a strategy. We'd like to use the law to strike down inequities like the one you just described. We want to attack the separate but equal system at its most vulnerable points. Oklahoma has a state-supported law school for white students, but not for blacks. That's something that should be changed."

"Sounds good," Ada said. She noticed that everyone in the room was staring at her. She felt as if they were sizing her up. "What do you want from me?"

"To challenge something in court, we need to file a lawsuit. To file a lawsuit, we need a plaintiff."

"What's a plaintiff?"

"An individual who has been wronged by the law. Or by the failure of the government to apply the law as it is written. That person files a lawsuit asking the courts to order the state to obey the law."

Ada's chin slowly rose. "What kind of . . . plaintiff do you need?"

"We need someone smart and accomplished. Someone who clearly would have been admitted to OU if they weren't black. We need someone with stamina—because this lawsuit is likely to drag on for a long time." He paused a moment. "And we need someone brave. Because this will not be easy."

"Maybe you should ask my brother, Lemuel, Ada said. "He's smart and brave. He fought in Europe in the war. And he was on the President's Honor Cabinet at Langston."

Ada's father laid his hand on the arm of her chair. "Lemuel has already had to delay his education three years while he was in the army. He's anxious to get on with his life." Her father stared directly into Ada's eyes. "We need someone with patience. Someone willing to delay her education for a good cause. This will be a long and bitter fight."

Ada could hardly believe what she was hearing. Could they possibly be suggesting—?

"I'm afraid you have me to blame for this, Ada," Mr. Dunjee said. "You made a big impression on me that day you came to my office. I saw how hard you had fought for something you believed in. And I saw a lot of fire in your eyes. We need that fire, Ada."

"H-Have you talked to my parents about this?" Ada asked.

"'Course they have," her mother said. "Do you think we'd be having this meeting if they hadn't?"

"And—what did they say?"

"They said we should talk to you directly," Dunjee explained.

"What I said," her father added, taking her by the hand, "was that they could search the whole world over and never find a plaintiff as good as my daughter. You've got good grades, lots of activities, lots of leadership experience. It's perfect. Perfect for them . . ." He hesitated. "And perfect for you."

"Perfect for me? How?"

Her father gave her hand a squeeze. "All your life you've had a big brain. Not to mention a big mouth." He grinned. "Now you have a chance to use both, in an important and historic way."

Ada's eyes started to itch. She looked away from him. She was determined to look grownup and mature. She did not want them to see her crying.

"Tell her about the difficulties, Roscoe," Ada's mother said. "And the dangers."

Ada's ears pricked up at the word "dangers."

"It's true," Dunjee said sadly. "It will be hard. You'll have to enroll at OU—but you won't be admitted. State law prevents any race mixing at state schools. So we'll have to go to court. And we'll lose."

What? Ada wondered if she'd heard right. *What was the point of filing a lawsuit if they were going to lose?*

"We'll lose, but that will give us the right to appeal. We'll be allowed to take our case to a higher court, the state Supreme Court."

"And that will go better?" Ada asked eagerly.

"No," Dunjee sighed wearily. "We'll lose there, too."

"Then what is the point of all this?"

"The point, Ada, is to get to Washington. We'll claim that Oklahoma is not obeying the United States Constitution. We'll appeal to the highest court in the country. The U.S. Supreme Court."

"And they'll have to take the case?"

"No. They get far more appeals than they can handle. They vote to decide whether to take a case."

"Then they might turn us down?"

Dr. Bullock set down his coffee cup. "That's a chance we have to take, my dear. But this is an important issue. There's a good chance they'll hear what we have to say."

"And if they do take the case, we'll finally win?"

There was a long silence that Ada did not like one bit. "We can't be sure how the Court will vote. But they have said that education in state schools can be separate only if it is equal. That's not being done here."

Mr. Dunjee cut in. "But the point, Ada, is that all these appeals will take a long time. Years. And during that time, you won't be able to go to school. If you go to school somewhere else, the Court will say your case is moot."

"What does that mean?"

"It means it doesn't matter any more—because you're in a different school. Once your case becomes moot, there's no more lawsuit."

Ada thought about that a long time. If she said yes, it might be years before she got to law school. Even longer before she graduated.

"The dangers, Roscoe," Ada's mother said firmly. "Don't forget to tell her about the dangers."

"I won't forget." Dunjee drew himself up. He looked at Ada sternly. "Ada, you've lived in a segregated city in a segregated state all your life."

"Yes, sir."

"I don't guess I have to tell you that there are . . . some people who don't want to see our people get equal rights."

"No, sir."

"In fact, there are some people who are willing to do . . . anything to prevent it."

"Yes, sir."

"Even resort to violence."

Ada stopped to catch her breath. Was he saying what she thought he was saying?

"Not all white people are like that, mind you. But there are some. This state has had the Ku Klux Klan since before statehood. For many years, the KKK practically ran the state government. It's better now, but there are still a lot of people in government determined to keep black people in their place. Bullies, basically. Narrow-minded, poorly educated bullies. From what I hear, you've run into a few of them."

"And made them wish they hadn't run into me," Ada replied firmly.

"Yes," he said, grinning. "There's that fire again. I love that fire."

"Get to the point, Roscoe," Dr. Bullock said, tapping his fingers on the arm of his chair.

Dunjee drew in a deep breath. "Ada, this is not the first lawsuit the NAACP has filed to challenge the separate but equal laws."

"It's isn't?"

"No. A man named Lloyd Gaines filed a similar suit a while back to get into school in Missouri."

"Did he win at the Supreme Court?"

"He never got to the Supreme Court."

"Why not?"

Dunjee bowed his head. "Lloyd Gaines spent years fighting. Years. He suffered not only legal problems but personal ones. Fought bigots and racists on a daily basis. Huge difficulties. And then one day—he disappeared."

Ada felt a sudden chill. "Disappeared?"

"We don't know what happened to him," Dr. Bullock explained. "But we have to assume . . ."

He fell silent before he finished his sentence, which was fine with Ada. She knew what he assumed.

Ada tried to remain brave. She could not help remembering, though, all the stories she had heard when she was growing up. She knew about the violence and death that so often happened whenever racists felt that black people "didn't know their place." It was frightening to think that she might become a target.

"So you see, Ada," Bullock continued, "this is a very serious decision. Serious in every possible way. You need to think about it before you give us an answer."

"What I said before," Dunjee added, "about what we need in a plaintiff—that wasn't quite complete. True, we need someone who is smart, someone who has earned the right to be in law school. And we need someone with patience. Someone who can fight a hard, long fight." He paused. "But what we need most of all is someone with courage."

Ada waited a long time before she spoke again. She saw concern in her parents' eyes. But she also remembered what they had taught her so many times in so many ways. She remembered that bully who had pushed Helen into the dirt and would've done worse—if Ada hadn't stood up to her. She remembered the conditions in the school she grew up in, the college she attended. She recalled how hard they'd had to fight for what little they had. She remembered how often in her short lifetime "separate but equal" had been proved a lie.

Most of all, she remembered what her father taught her. "Always stand up for what you believe," he had said, time and time again. "If it's worth having, it's worth fighting for."

Ada held out her hand to Mr. Dunjee. "I'll do it." She said. She shook his hand firmly. "I'm your plaintiff."

7

ENROLLMENT DAY

January 14, 1946 was a cold, blustery Oklahoma winter day. Mr. Bullock and Mr. Dunjee picked up Ada and drove her to Norman. They went to the admissions office, but circled the block several times because they could not find a place to park. Finally, Dunjee parked on the side of the street in a place he knew was not designated for parking.

"We won't be here long," he muttered, as he locked the car. They walked together to the office of the dean of admissions. He was a kind man who seemed to expect them. Ada realized he must have known they were coming. He reviewed Ada's college transcript and said that she met all the qualifications for admission to the law school. "Well," he added, "all the academic qualifications."

After that, Ada and her two escorts walked to the office of Dr. George L. Cross, the president of the university.

"Ada, are you nervous?" Dunjee asked.

"A little bit," she answered truthfully. It was hard applying for something when you knew you were going to be rejected.

"Well, a little nervousness is natural," Dunjee said. Then he added, with a twinkle in his eye, "But I expect some of the people here will be more nervous than you when they find out why you're here." Ada felt her knees trembling as she approached the President's office. She was very nervous. Of course, she had visited the president at Langston many times. But now she was going to see the famous George L. Cross! Even though he was a relatively young man, he had already made many important improvements at OU. He was influencing higher education all over the state. She knew her father admired him.

What will Dr. Cross think of me? she wondered. Would he approve of what she was doing? Or would he think she was "uppity," a young troublemaker who did not know her place?

Ada was amazed that they could get in so readily to meet the president. Again, she realized that he must have been expecting her. He had a kind face that immediately put Ada at ease. He wore round owl eyeglasses and his black hair was slicked back. Ada was afraid he might be angry to see a young woman who could only represent a lot of trouble to him.

She had no reason to worry. He was relaxed and friendly. Mr. Dunjee introduced Ada. He bragged about her many accomplishments, then bragged about her father, the prominent minister. "Ada wishes to enter the law school at the University of Oklahoma," he explained. "She will commute daily from Oklahoma City."

No one had to explain to Dr. Cross why she would not live in Norman. Norman had a horrible reputation for its treatment of black people. The city's laws forbade blacks to be out after dark. Some of those who had been found there after dark disappeared and were never seen again. No restaurant in Norman would serve blacks. No hotel or motel would accept them as guests.

Dr. Cross examined Ada's transcript. "Very impressive," he murmured, turning the pages. "An honor student. I like honor students."

"She excels in everything she does," Dr. Bullock explained.

"I can see that." Dr. Cross laid down the transcript. "I don't see how anyone could question this young woman's scholastic qualifications. I see that the dean of admissions thought the same thing."

Ada beamed with pride. Dr. Cross seemed so positive, so encouraging, she almost began to believe that she would be admitted after all.

The room fell silent. Ada had the impression that Dr. Cross knew what was going to happen next, but was not anxious to do it.

"Well?" Dunjee said, urging him on.

Dr. Cross nodded. "A decision must be made regarding Mrs. Fisher's admission. Being the President of the University, I suppose that duty falls to me."

Dr. Cross explained that many people at OU would be happy to admit Ada and other black students. Unfortunately, the Oklahoma state Constitution did not allow the mixing of races in schools. Therefore, the state board of regents had issued an order directing all college presidents at white schools to refuse to admit black students.

Dr. Cross showed Ada a copy of the resolution. "Whether I like it or not," he explained, "they are my superiors. I have no choice but to deny your application."

Ada tried not to show her disappointment. Instead, she remembered what she and her advisors had talked about before they arrived. "Dr. Cross," she said, "would you mind explaining what you have just told me in writing?"

Dr. Cross smiled. "I'll be happy to give you anything you need." Ada had requested a letter for a good reason. If they went to court and complained that Ada had not been admitted, the university officials might say she had been turned down for reasons other than her race. They might say that she was turned down because Langston was not an accredited university. They might claim that her Langston grades were not the equivalent of grades from other schools. None of these excuses would have violated the law. For that matter, they might give no reason at all. If they did that, Ada would be forced to prove in court that she had been turned down because she was black.

Ada knew Dr. Cross did not have to give her a written explanation.

In fact, it would be much easier for him if he did not. Nonetheless, he called his stenographer into the room and dictated a letter. He dictated it with such clarity and precision that Ada was certain he had thought about it in advance. "The dean of admissions has found that you are qualified to attend law school at this university," Dr. Cross dictated. "Still, I must deny your admission for the following two reasons. First, state law makes it illegal for black students to attend white colleges. I would be committing a misdemeanor offense if I admitted you to this college. Any teacher who taught you would also be violating the law. Second, the board of regents has instructed me to deny admission to all black students. That applies even when the student is qualified to attend, as you clearly are."

Ada knew the letter was exactly the ammunition they would need in court. She was disappointed that she was denied admission—even though everyone had told her she would be. But she knew the battle was just beginning. They all shook hands and left the office. To Ada's surprise, there were photographers waiting for her outside. She also met student members of a group dedicated to improving race relations. Mr. Dunjee announced that they would be filing a lawsuit to fight the wrongful rejection of Ada's application to law school. He also thanked Dr. Cross for his kindness and courtesy.

Many pictures were taken. Afterward, some of the students and faculty took them out for lunch. They ate sack lunches on the campus lawn, since no Norman restaurant would serve blacks. Ada was pleased to see that so many of the white students and faculty were friendly. Once again she was reminded of her mother's words. Not all white people are against us. Not even most. Just some.

At the same time, Ada knew that she would have to be cautious about what even a few might do.

On their way out, they were all pleased to see that Mr. Dunjee had not gotten a parking ticket. They were not in trouble with the law.

Not yet, anyway.

8

THE "CIRCUS" COURT

After Ada's application for law school was denied, her lawyers filed an application for a *writ of mandamus*. That, Ada learned, is an order from a judge to a government official requiring them to perform an official duty. In this case, they wanted the local Norman judge to order the dean of admissions at OU to admit Ada. A date was set for the formal hearing on the application.

Everything changed for Ada. Suddenly it seemed as if everyone was talking about the skinny black girl from Chickasha who was demanding an equal education. Her picture was in newspapers and magazines. When she walked down the street, she could tell people were talking about her. Sometimes they would point or whisper in low tones. Ada was not sure if she should be proud or worried. Maybe a little bit of both.

Ada received many phone calls from near and far. Most of them were supportive. A few people expressed concerns for her safety. No one had forgotten about Lloyd Gaines or his mysterious disappearance. They did not want to see anything bad happen to Ada—or her family, her husband, or her home. Ada could be certain that her neighbors were behind her. Back home in the black part of Chickasha, everyone was proud of her. They supported her in any way that they could. Her father beamed with pride when he saw her picture in the newspaper.

He cut out the entire article and put it on his desk. He told everyone he saw about his strong, smart, courageous daughter.

One day, not long after the lawsuit was filed, Ada visited an optometrist. She had been a reader all her life, but it was getting harder for her to focus on the letters. She realized she needed glasses. She did not know the white man who examined her eyes. He recognized her from the newspapers. "You're that little girl who's trying to get into OU, aren't you?" He asked, during the examination.

Ada was not sure anyone over twenty-one could be considered a "little girl," especially when she was married. "Yes," she answered politely. "That's me."

"I went to school in another state, up north. I had classes with colored people." He adjusted the frames on her new glasses. Then he added, "I'm not saying whether I liked it."

"Well," Ada replied, "the black students you went to class with probably didn't ask if you liked it, so neither will I." Ada suspected that this doctor did not make anything easier for those black students. *But*, she thought, *at least they got to go to school.*

While Ada awaited her court date, dear Dr. Bullock passed away. She had known for some time that his health was failing. She had come to care for him dearly. He had been so important to the black Chickasha community. Ada knew that she owed him a great deal. Almost everyone in the neighborhood turned out for his funeral. Many people were nice enough to tell Ada they knew Dr. Bullock was proud of her. In fact, they felt that Ada was continuing the work he had begun. Ada was sad to see this great man pass. But she was pleased to think that she might carry on his important legacy.

The first thing Ada learned about lawsuits was that they attracted a lot of attention. The second thing she learned was that they cost a lot of money. The NAACP was supporting her, but they could not solely fund a suit they expected to take years and go all the way to Washington, D.C. If she were going to continue the suit, they would have to raise some money.

"Ada," Mr. Dunjee said one day at her home, "since you're not going to be able to go to school for a while, how would you like to go on a little road trip?"

Ada was intrigued. "Where would we go?"

A smile played on his lips. "Everyplace where people have money."

As it turned out, Mr. Dunjee's little road trip was a speaking tour that took Ada to more than a dozen cities in Oklahoma, then several other states. They spoke in schools and churches and community centers. Sometimes they spoke outside in tents. Usually, Mr. Dunjee would speak first. He talked about the important work the NAACP was doing. He reminded everyone how important it was to bring equality to all people.

Then he would talk about Ada's case. He would explain why it was important, not just to Ada, but to all black Americans who wanted to educate themselves or work in a profession. When he was finished, he would introduce Ada.

At first, Ada hated the idea of speaking in front of other people. She had always been shy. Her knees would wobble as she walked to the podium. Her voice would become so dry she could barely speak. She might be a "smart mouth" when she was with people she knew, but speaking to large groups of strangers made her nervous.

As always, Ada forced herself to do what she knew was right. Over time, she became a more polished speaker. She chose to let Mr. Dunjee do most of the talking about the legal battle. She talked about her family and what she had learned from them. She talked about the support she had received from her hometown community. She always ended with her father's words. "If it's worth having," she would tell them, "it's worth fighting for."

In 1946, the NAACP held their state convention in Chickasha. Ada was the guest of honor and the keynote speaker. She was surprised to find a large group of young white people in the audience. After she finished speaking, one of them came up to meet her.

"My name is Ben Blackstock," he said, extending his hand. "I go to school at OU. So do my friends. My brother is in law school there."

"Very pleased to meet you," Ada said, shaking his hand. "We just want you to know that we would be honored to have you at our school," Ben said. His friends shook their heads in agreement. "We are solidly behind you. We believe you could be a great asset to OU."

Ada felt as if someone had taken her breath away. She was touched that these students had come so far to lend their support. They seemed like fine people. She hoped that one day she could be a fellow student.

Afterward, Mr. Dunjee greeted Ada with a broad grin. "You did a fine job, Ada."

"I did my best. Those people were very kind."

"And very generous. We raised a good deal of money for your legal fund. I think now we'll be able to pay all the filing fees and court costs. We can also pay the expenses for your lawyers."

"That's good news," Ada said. "Is that why you've got that big grin on your face?"

"No," Dunjee said. He handed Ada a copy of the morning newspaper. "This is."

Ada scanned the paper quickly. It was open to the page that listed the overseas troops who had arrived in New York City. From there they would be sent to other military bases throughout the country. Quickly, her eyes scanned down to the "F" column . . .

Warren was coming home! Ada was so excited she threw her arms around Mr. Dunjee and hugged him. He had been away for so long! It was wonderful to know that he had arrived safely back in the United States.

"Do you know where he is now?" Ada asked.

Dunjee nodded. "He's at Fort Chaffee, in Arkansas. They're processing his discharge."

Discharge! "You mean—"

"I sure do, Ada. He's on his way here now."

By the time Ada returned home, Warren was waiting for her.

Ada was happier with her husband at home, but she was anxious for her court date. Why did everything have to take so long? Finally, Mr. Dunjee told her that her case had been set for trial in July.

"And the even better news," he explained, "is that Amos Hall has agreed to be your lawyer."

Ada knew who Amos Hall was. He was well respected in the black community. Many times he had represented black men who had been charged with a crime primarily because of their race. Sometimes he was able to set innocent men free. She knew that having a man with such a distinguished reputation could only help her case.

"But that's not all," Mr. Dunjee said. "Amos feels that he should have co-counsel. That means another lawyer helping him out."

Two lawyers! That sounded wonderful. Ada was glad she had spent so much time raising funds. "Did he have anyone in mind?"

"Ada," he said slowly, "how would you feel about being represented by . . . Thurgood Marshall?"

If Ada's jaw had not been attached, it would have dropped to the floor. Thurgood Marshall! The most famous black lawyer in the United States? The man who had so inspired her when he spoke in Chickasha all those years ago? He was as a large part of the reason she wanted to be a lawyer. And now he was going to help her in her fight to become one. It was just too incredible to be believed.

A week later, Ada traveled to Oklahoma City to meet Mr. Marshall. He was joining Dunjee, Hall, and several others to plan their strategy for the case. Ada felt the same nervousness in her stomach she used to feel about public speaking. Thurgood Marshall!

Finally, Mr. Marshall arrived. He was a tall man, and as handsome and charming as she remembered. After Marshall entered the room, Dunjee introduced them. "This is the young lady," he said.

Ada wasn't sure how to behave around such a great man. She held out her hand. She was so nervous it trembled. Marshall immediately put her at ease. He took her hand, shook it, then pulled her close and gave her a big hug. They sat down and Marshall started telling stories. He told Ada about his life, growing up in the south, dealing with the Ku Klux Klan and other hate groups. He told her about having to outrun a lynch mob late one night in a small town in Tennessee. He told her about being harassed by southern policemen and sheriffs when he was helping black people exercise their right to vote.

No matter how serious his stories were, however, Ada noticed that Marshall almost always had a smile on his face. Even the grimmest anecdote ended up having a punch line. Ada knew right away that she would like working with him.

At last, the day came. It was July in Oklahoma, and the courthouse in Norman did not have air conditioning. It was hot, humid and crowded. Even before she got inside the courtroom, Ada knew this was going to be a special day. The streets were packed. Apparently some of the schools had canceled classes so that students could attend the spectacle. The bailiff had to turn many spectators away. Far more people wanted to watch than the tiny courtroom could hold. They were curious to see what would happen. Many had never seen a black man in the courtroom, except as a defendant.

With so many people crowded into a tiny space on a hot day, it was no surprise that the courtroom was noisy. People of all ages were packed into the tiny room. Some of them even had cameras. There was shouting and laughing and backslapping.

"Don't they know the difference between a courtroom and a carnival?" Hall grumped.

"I think the circuit court is turning into a circus court," Dunjee told Ada with a wink.

As soon as Ada entered, however, the courtroom fell silent. The whispering stopped. Ada felt as if everyone were staring at her—and she was probably right. She knew many of the people in the room. She had met most of the reporters since the day she applied for admission. She knew lots of the NAACP people from all the public speaking she had done to raise money. There were people present she did not know, though. Many of them did not smile as she passed.

Ada took her seat at the plaintiff's table and waited for the judge to arrive. There would be no jury. As her lawyers had explained, juries were only called when there were facts in dispute. In this case, there was no argument about what happened. Ada had applied for law school at OU and they had turned her down. The only question was whether that was legal. Since it was a legal question, a judge would decide it.

A bailiff announced Judge Ben Williams. He entered the courtroom. A lawyer from the attorney general's office, Fred Hansen, represented the state. He was helped by a man named Maurice Merrill who was the dean of OU's law school. Ada was amazed. This man might have been her teacher. Instead, he was helping the government keep her out of school.

Amos Hall was the first to speak to the judge. He did exactly what they had planned. He calmly and concisely explained why Ada should have been admitted to the law school. "According to the Supreme Court," he said to the judge, "the government can keep black students out of one school only if there is another school they can attend. Another school of equal quality. This is called the 'separate but equal' rule. What's important to remember, your honor, is that the two parts go together. There can't be any separate unless there's also equal. You can't have one without the other."

The judge was silent. Amos Hall continued. "In Oklahoma, we have used tax dollars to create a place where white students can study law. There is no equal opportunity for black students. That's not separate but equal. That's just separate." He pointed toward Ada. "This fine young student applied in a timely fashion to the University of Oklahoma. Her transcript is excellent. The dean of admissions said she is qualified. The president of the university said she would have been admitted, if not for her race. Now that's just wrong."

Judge Williams asked him a question. "Mr. Hall, surely the state can't afford to start a separate graduate school for blacks in every field of study? Today, we're talking about a law school. Tomorrow it might be an engineering school, or a medical school, or something else. It's too expensive."

Mr. Hall nodded. "The solution, your honor, is to let black students attend the schools we already have. That won't cost anything. But if we insist on having separate schools, we're going to need a separate school for every field in which we have a school for white students. Since we don't have a law school for black students, your honor, the court should issue the writ ordering OU to admit this student."

Ada listened to his clear, persuasive argument. How could anyone disagree with what he said? And yet, she could tell the judge was not sympathetic. She remembered what Thurgood Marshall had said years earlier about the need for soldiers in the battle for equality. She wanted to become a lawyer more than ever.

Dean Merrill spoke on behalf of the state. He was also smart and well spoken. "We all know the law on 'separate but equal,' your honor," he said, tucking a thumb in his watch pocket as he spoke, "but that's not the only law. The Constitution of the great state of Oklahoma says that it is illegal for black students to attend white schools. It would be illegal for OU's dean of admission to grant this woman's application. They have come into this courtroom to ask you to order something illegal."

Merrill smiled at Ada. "I'm glad this young lady wants to improve herself. I know there are schools outside Oklahoma where she could get a legal education. What she should have done is tell the state board of regents she wanted to study law. If she had, they might've been able to start one up at Langston, where it would be legal for her to go to school. They might have been able to arrange some financing to send her out of state."

Ada saw Hall and Marshall exchanging a frown. They had anticipated this response. They did not believe for a minute that the board of regents would have done anything to help her. Besides, they did not want the state to start creating second-rate graduate schools. They wanted to integrate the schools that already existed.

Amos Hall returned to the podium. "Have you seen the Oklahoma City newspaper?" he asked. "They've conducted a little poll. Seems most of the students at OU believe Ada should be admitted. But here's the remarkable thing. Most Oklahomans favor letting her in, too. Why are we saying no to her? She has the grades. She followed the correct procedures. The people of this great state want her there. Why hasn't she been admitted?"

Hall's voice rose. "The law is supposed to express the will of the people. This is a good country with good people. That's why we passed the fourteenth amendment, so everyone would be treated equally. So every person in this great land can have the chance to be the best person they can be. So I ask you, your honor, to do what we all know is right." He laid his hand on Ada's shoulder. "Let this smart young woman go to law school."

Ada's lawyers had told her what the result of the hearing would be before it even started. Still, it hurt when the judge reentered the courtroom that afternoon and read his decision. "The court uses the *writ of mandamus*," Judge Williams said, reading from his prepared opinion, "to compel agents of the state government to obey the law—not to disobey it. It would be a gross injustice to issue a writ ordering someone to do something that is absolutely forbidden by the Oklahoma Constitution. Therefore, the plaintiff's request for a writ of mandamus is denied."

Ada and her legal team drove back home immediately. They knew that it would not be smart to be in Norman after dark. "I know you told me we were going to lose," Ada said, "But it still hurts when it happens."

"Hoops!" Amos Hall said loudly. "Hoops!"

9

THE MEANING OF EQUAL

Ada wondered if she had heard him correctly. "I don't understand."

"We're jumping through hoops, just like trained animals in a circus. We knew we were going to lose here. But we had to lose here before we could appeal to the Oklahoma Supreme Court. And the chances are, we'll lose there, too. That's okay. We have to show that a lower court has made a mistake before we can appeal to a higher court. These are the hoops we have to jump through to get to the United States Supreme Court."

"And that's when we'll win?" Ada asked anxiously.

Hall took a deep breath. "That's where we have a fighting chance."

Ada and her lawyers appealed the court's decision the very next day. While they waited for a court date, Warren went to work for a company that made powdered eggs—which he hated. Ada was not able to go to school because of the lawsuit, but she managed to find work when she could. The community continued to support her. More than once she was reminded how important it is to have loyal family and friends.

In September, while she was still waiting to appear before the Oklahoma Supreme Court, a tragedy occurred, one she had long dreaded. While her father was in Oklahoma City on a business meeting, he suffered a heart attack. Ada, her mother, Lemuel, and

Warren raced to Oklahoma City. By the time they arrived, he was already dead. He was lying on a divan, surrounded by several of the ministers attending the meeting. "It happened very suddenly," one kindly minister explained. "I don't think he felt any pain."

Ada felt lost and alone without her father. Of course he was seventy years old, and Ada knew that eventually his time would come. That did not make it any easier to bear, though. She missed him terribly.

A few days later, his funeral was held in Oklahoma City at the state headquarters of his church. Another memorial service was held in Chickasha. Ada was amazed by all the people who turned out to pay their last respects.

"Your father was a great man," one of his fellow ministers told Ada, after the funeral.

"I know that, sir," Ada answered, staring at the ground. "A great man who accomplished many great deeds. A brave man, full of strength and moral fiber."

"Yes, sir."

"He had a great deal to be proud about." The minister paused. "But do you know what he was proudest of?"

Ada looked up slowly.

"He never stopped talking about you. Your case, your fight. Your courage. Your determination to see justice done."

"R-really?"

"Oh, my, yes. He was so proud of you. He said, 'I like to think I've done some important work in my time. But what my Ada is doing—that's important. That little girl of mine is going to change the face of the world.'"

Ada didn't know what to say, so she remained silent.

"I know this has hit you hard, Ada. But you stay strong, you hear me? Your father wasn't the only person rooting for you. We all are."

Ada felt tears welling up in her eyes. "Thank you." "Don't you fool yourself into thinking that you've lost your father's support," the minister said. He put a finger under her chin and lifted it so she could see his eyes. "He's just moved to a different place. But he's still watching over you. And he always will be."

The Oklahoma Supreme Court heard Ada's case on March 4, 1947, at the Capitol building in Oklahoma City. There was no jury. The lawyers would make their legal arguments directly to the Court. This time, though, there were nine judges, and they interrupted the lawyers any time they wished. Ada thought it seemed rude, but being a judge on the Supreme Court was a lifetime appointment. So Ada supposed you could get away with doing about anything you wanted to do.

Every one of the nine members of the Court was a white man. Still, Amos Hall assured Ada, most of the justices wanted to do the right thing. They tried to apply the law fairly. The problem was, at least in this case, the law of Oklahoma was against them.

As before, Dean Merrill and Assistant Attorney General Hansen represented the state. And also as before, the courtroom was packed. Reporters, lawyers, students, and many other interested people filled the room. Ada had the same feeling she'd had before—many of the people supported her, but some did not. By the time the case was ready to be heard, it was standing room only. Ada was glad that this time the hearing was not in the heat of the summer.

Amos Hall was the first to speak. "If it please the Court." Again, he argued that the failure to admit Ada to law school violated the equal protection guarantee in the fourteenth amendment. "Hundreds of white students have graduated from OU's law school. Most of them didn't have a record half as good as my client's academic record. When the state supports a school that educates some students, but refuses to educate others, it is not treating all people equally."

One of the judges, associate Justice Earl Welch, interrupted. "If the state of Oklahoma is guilty of violating the U.S. Constitution now, does that mean it was guilty of violating the Constitution in 1908 when it passed these laws that forbid mixing the races?"

Ada was not a lawyer, but she knew what the answer to this question had to be. Still, she noticed that Hall thought carefully before answering. "Yes, your honor, the state was wrong in 1908 and it has been wrong every year since."

Justice Welch was not satisfied. "But the laws of Oklahoma require the two races to be kept separate."

"Yes, sir, they do. And that law violates the U.S. Constitution."

"What about the possibility that the board of regents might provide money? Then your client can attend law school in another state."

Hall spoke forcefully. If they lost this point, they lost the case. "Your honor, how can we pretend that sending someone away to another state is equal to giving them an education right here at home? Even if the board offered to pay for tuition—which it has not done— few could afford to go to school so far away."

Justice Welch kept probing. "Are you saying, then, that when the state set up a law school for white students, it should have set up a separate school for Negroes?"

"Yes, your honor. The law requires it."

"And any time the state sets up any other kind of school or graduate program, it has to set up a second school for Negroes?"

"Absolutely."

"Do you have any idea what that would cost?"

"I think it would be very expensive," Hall conceded. "It would be much simpler, and smarter, to admit black students to the colleges we have."

After the judges were finished questioning Amos Hall, it was Mr. Hansen's turn to speak. He referred to Thurgood Marshall as an "outside troublemaker." He called the papers filed in Ada's case "the New York brief." Ada could not understand what difference it could make to the judges where a lawyer came from or where papers were written. Why wasn't he talking about the law?

"Don't let their elegant words about fairness and equality fool you," Hansen said. "This is not about whether one little girl goes to law school. This is a concentrated New York NAACP plan to break down segregation—which has been the law of this state for as long as this state has existed. What business do these New York people have telling us how to run our state?"

Before they came to court, Ada had been instructed by her lawyers not to show any expression on her face during the hearing. No matter what was said, they cautioned, you must remain calm. Don't react. It was a good thing they told her, too. Because right then, she had a strong desire to stick out her tongue.

"If this young woman had informed the board of regents that she wanted to go to law school, we might have been able to arrange something. But she did not. It would be expensive and foolhardy for the state to start building schools just in case someday a black student wishes to attend them. But she never contacted the board of regents. She simply applied to a school where she knew she could not go. Instead of seeking a legal solution, she sought an illegal one."

At last it was time for Thurgood Marshall to speak. Ada marveled at how calm he was. He acted as if he had not heard any of the things Hansen had said about him or the organization he represented. He smiled at the Court and began his argument. Before he could finish a sentence, though, Justice Welch interrupted him.

"Is it true what the agent of the attorney general's office said, Mr. Marshall? Are you here to bring down segregation? Not just in schools but in every part of Oklahoma life?"

Marshall kept smiling. The question did not faze him in the least. "It is true, your honor, that I personally am opposed to segregation. If you had grown up where I did, or seen some of the injustices I have seen, you might oppose segregation, too. But segregation is not the issue the Court is considering today. This distinguished court has been asked to decide a much more narrow issue. Is the state of Oklahoma denying my client's constitutional right to equal protection under the law?"

"I've read your New York brief," Justice Welch said. "I know you're going to say that any segregation of the races violates the Constitution."

Ada realized that a lawyer had to work hard, and study, and be smart—but the most important thing a lawyer had to do was keep cool. "Our brief, your honor, was written and researched by Mr. Amos Hall in Tulsa, with the help of lawyers in Oklahoma City and Chickasha. It was printed in New York because it was less expensive to do it there. But that is not what this case is about. These are distractions designed to keep the Court from focusing on the main issue. Does the state's failure to provide a legal education to Ada Sipuel Fisher violate her Constitutional rights?"

"And you're going to claim that it does," Justice Welch said, "even though we've been doing things this way for the last forty years?"

Marshall laid his hands calmly on the podium. "Does the Constitution apply now, your honors, or will we have to wait another forty years? How long must we wait until the fourteenth amendment is more than just words? How long will it be before the law of the land is actually enforced?"

Ada was not surprised at the ruling. Just like the last time, her lawyers had warned her that the Court would probably rule against her.

They did.

Dunjee came by Ada's home to explain the ruling to her. "It was actually better than we expected, Ada. The Court totally rejected all that nonsense about the state providing money to send you out of state. They agreed that the equal protection clause of the Constitution requires the state to provide equal facilities within the state."

"Then why didn't we win?"

Dunjee sighed. "The judges said that you should have given the board of regents notice that you wanted to attend law school. So they could create one for you."

"This just makes me so . . . angry! It's not fair!"

"I know, Ada. I know. We're filing a *writ of certiorari.*"

"What's that?"

"It means we're appealing to the United States Supreme Court—the ultimate authority on what the Constitution means, including the fourteenth amendment."

"And how do we know they will rule any differently than the other two courts?"

"We don't know how they will rule," he admitted. "But we know we're right. So we can't stop trying. No matter how long and hard the battle."

Ada could almost hear her father's voice as he spoke. "If it's worth having, it's worth fighting for," she said.

"That's right, dear. And that's why we're going to Washington."

10

ADA GOES TO WASHINGTON

The decision of the Oklahoma Supreme Court attracted attention all across the nation. Ada was glad she had her mother, her brother and sister, and her loving husband to support her. Courage, though, as her father had often told her, was not something someone can give you. Either you have it or you don't. Ada decided that she was going to have it—if not for her own sake, then for her father's.

Some of the letters she received were very complimentary. They were kind and often offered support. There were others, however, that were less kind. Some of them used foul language, which Ada quickly learned was the surest sign of either a bad education or a stupid brain. One letter called her a "stringy-haired, tall, skinny, sallow-faced negress" and suggested that, instead of going to law school, she should go back to "the jungles of Africa." Ada did not mind so much being called skinny, but she wondered what her hair had to do with anything.

One letter arrived addressed simply to: *Ada Sipuel, nigger, Oklahoma.* By that time, Ada was so famous that the post office knew where to deliver it, even though it did not have an address. Several of the letters threatened that, if she ever did get into OU, people would be waiting to show her what happens to uppity colored girls who don't know their place. The OU student newspaper ran another poll to ask its students whether they thought Ada should be admitted. Ada was pleased to see that most of the students did. In fact, most of the students supported admitting black students in any case. Some of them wrote editorials supporting Ada in the student newspaper. They sounded like kind, smart people. More than ever, Ada wanted to attend OU. She knew it was a fine university. She wanted the chance to study with these bright students.

The hardest part for Ada was waiting. She could not continue her studies. She was constantly working to raise funds. Finally, nearly two years after she first applied to law school, the U.S. Supreme Court accepted her appeal and set a date for hearing her case: January 8, 1948.

It was a bitterly cold day in Washington, D.C., as Ada walked up the huge marble steps that led to the magnificent Supreme Court building. Amos Hall and Thurgood Marshall were with her. When she saw the huge imposing marble building, she could not help but worry. Had she been foolish to attempt to get into law school? Was it only a dream to think that equal might really, finally, mean "equal?"

As she climbed the steps, Ada noticed the words carved into the triangular front façade of the Supreme Court building: Equal Justice under Law.

Ada recalled what her mother had told her so many years before about the Whites Only sign—that it had two sides.

She liked this sign much better. The building said Equal Justice on the outside. She was counting on it saying the same thing on the inside.

Ada had never seen anything like the interior of the Supreme Court building. The walls and floors were made of white marble inlaid with black, imported from Europe. The red carpet was thick and plush. She almost felt guilty about walking on it. The corridors were lined with uniformed soldiers standing at attention. She was in one of the most important buildings in the American government.

I've waited two years to see this, Ada thought. *And it was worth it. No matter what happens. It was worth it.*

Thurgood Marshall escorted her inside the court chamber where the oral argument would be held. It was nothing like the courtrooms she had seen in Oklahoma. She remembered the scenes in Mark Twain's *The Prince and the Pauper* when Tom sees the inside of the palace for the first time. He must have felt as she did now. All the pews, chairs, and wall hangings were carved from mahogany and other rich polished woods. Beyond the bar that separated the gallery from the judge's chamber, there were nine large leather padded chairs. A red curtain hung behind the chairs.

The bailiff called the court into session. They all rose to their feet. Then, one by one, the nine justices of the Supreme Court entered from behind the curtain. The Chief Justice announced the name of the case and invited the lawyers to step forward. Each side would be given one hour to argue their case. Then the justices would retire to make their decision. Thurgood Marshall spoke first. He was just as eloquent as he had always been. He argued that separate but equal could not possibly apply when the state was not even providing a separate school, much less an equal one.

"The time has come," Marshall argued, "to realize that no matter how much money is spent, or how hard people try, separate will never be equal. Maybe 'separate but equal' seemed like a workable solution eighty years ago. But it has only resulted in unnecessary expense and hardship. The fourteenth amendment guarantees equal treatment.

Those words will never be a reality so long as 'separate but equal' is the law of the land."

Marshall was doing exactly what Dean Merrill had accused him of doing at the Oklahoma Supreme Court. He was trying to end segregation once and for all. Ada noticed that he did it boldly and confidently, as he seemed to do everything.

She noticed something else, too. Although the justices of the Supreme Court had the right to interrupt at any time, they did not interrupt Thurgood Marshall. Not even once. The expressions on their faces did not tell Ada what they might be thinking. She was certain, though, that they respected this man. They were listening carefully to what he had to say.

For the first time, Ada allowed herself to think that this fall she might actually be attending law school.

When Hansen and Merrill spoke on behalf of the state of Oklahoma, they were barely able to finish a sentence. The justices of the Supreme Court constantly interrupted them. They tried to understand how Oklahoma could be honoring its obligation to educate its people equally when they did not even offer a law school black students could attend. They also did not appear impressed by the argument that Ada should have notified the board of regents.

When Dean Merrill argued that mixing races at college would violate Oklahoma law, the judges seemed frustrated. Did Oklahoma have the right to pass laws that violated the United States Constitution? Didn't the U.S. Supreme Court have the obligation to invalidate any laws that violated the U.S. Constitution?

Justice William O. Douglas interrupted Merrill. "Are you suggesting that the board of regents do not know this young woman wishes to attend law school?"

Merrill cleared his throat. "No formal notice was ever given."

"That wasn't my question, counsel. Do they know?"

"Sir, the proper procedure for communicating with the board of regents was not followed."

"But they know, don't they?" Justice Douglas seemed increasingly frustrated with his inability to get a straight answer. "She tried to enroll two years ago. Surely by now they've figured out that she wants to go to law school?"

"Well, your honor—"

"But they've done nothing to make that happen."

"Your honor, the laws of the state of Oklahoma require that certain procedures must be followed. Once the board is properly notified of the plaintiff's desires, they will take action accordingly."

Justice Douglas fell back into his leather chair. "At the rate the state of Oklahoma is moving, the plaintiff will be an old lady before she'll be able to practice law."

Ada covered her hand with her mouth and tried not to laugh. Justice Robert Jackson followed with more questions. "It has been two years since she applied to law school, counselor. Has the state done anything to remedy this problem?"

Merrill cleared his throat. Ada thought he looked even more nervous. "Your honor, the state does not believe it has a problem."

Justice Hugo Black jumped into the debate. "Counsel, I want to know whether the board of regents has done anything to satisfy this young woman's desire to attend law school."

"Well . . ." Merrill said, "the board has not taken any . . . direct action."

"Are you saying it has taken indirect action?"

Merrill fingered his collar. "Your honor, the regents do no have any reason to believe that the plaintiff would wish to attend another law school. We have only been given notice that she would like to attend the University of Oklahoma—which is illegal."

Ada was pleased when Justice Felix Frankfurter joined the argument. He was a famous man. She had studied him in school.

She knew he had a distinguished career as a lawyer. He helped many important social causes during the Depression years and had spoken out against the unfairness of the trial of Sacco and Vanzetti. President Franklin D. Roosevelt appointed him to the Supreme Court.

"It would seem to me," Justice Frankfurter said, fingering his big bushy eyebrows, "that nothing has been done to honor the principle of 'separate but equal' established by this Court. I would like to explore the possible alternatives." Fred Hansen was now taking his turn to speak before the Court. "Yes, sir."

"Would the state be willing to admit this young woman to law school for the fall term if it were ordered to do so by this Court?"

Hansen thought before answering. "I suppose we would have no choice, sir, if a direct order came from the U.S. Supreme Court. But it would violate the laws of the state of Oklahoma." Frankfurter nodded thoughtfully. "Could a separate course of study be established at the existing law school? The state could reduce costs by using the same facilities and library and instructors."

"I suppose that could be done, your honor." Hansen hesitated. "But it would still violate the laws of the state of Oklahoma."

"Could the plaintiff be admitted to the current law school temporarily, until a separate school can be established?"

Again, Hansen answered that it would be possible—but illegal.

"Does the Oklahoma board of regents have the authority to enact any of these solutions?"

"Yes, sir."

"And so far—it has done none of them."

Hansen did not have to answer. Everyone knew that it had not.

Instead, Hansen said, "Your honors, segregation has been the law in our state for decades. The plaintiff is simply unwilling to accept our long-settled policy."

Well, Ada thought, *that's the first correct thing he's said all day.*

"But counsel," Justice Jackson added, "she doesn't have to accept any policy if it violates her constitutional rights. No matter how long it has been the settled policy."

Ada loved listening to these lawyers debate the issues. Even the lawyers who opposed her application were smart. She could admire their education and preparation. What she loved most, though, was that the important questions were finally being asked. They were talking about equality, education, fairness—all the issues the previous courts had ignored.

Ada noticed that the justices of the U.S. Supreme Court were careful to ask questions without expressing opinions. She knew that was established judicial conduct, but it left her unsure what they were thinking.

When it was over, her lawyers expressed optimism. Marshall took encouragement from the fact that they did not seem to disagree with anything he said. But he also cautioned Ada that their silence was no guarantee of a favorable result.

Even after waiting so long, Ada did not know what the Supreme Court justices thought—or how long it would take them to decide.

11

INSTANT

As it turned out, it took the Supreme Court exactly four days. Because OU's semester was about to start, the U.S. Supreme Court issued a speedy, one-page order. It was unanimous—meaning all nine justices had agreed. The Supreme Court said that Ada was "entitled to secure legal education afforded by a state institution." The Court ordered the state to provide her an education "in conformity with the equal protection clause of the fourteenth amendment." They said that the state must do it just as quickly as it would for applicants of any other race.

Ada and her lawyers celebrated when they heard the news. "We won!" Ada said. They all exchanged hugs and handshakes. "We finally won!"

Mr. Dunjee was almost as exited as Ada. "I knew you could do it," he said, beaming proudly. "Knew it from the start." Amos Hall was just as excited the rest of them. They all celebrated with a big dinner in Washington.

Ada noticed that Thurgood Marshall was quieter than everyone else. He was obviously happy. Still, she could see that something was bothering him.

"What's wrong?" she asked. "Isn't this the end of the battle? Haven't we won?"

"Perhaps," Marshall said cautiously. "But I've fought enough battles to know it's best to be careful about declaring a victory." "But—the Supreme Court said they had to let me go to law school."

"Yes, Ada, they did." He paused. "But they did not strike down Oklahoma's segregation laws. They did not strike down 'separate but equal.' That could create some problems for you."

"What should I do?" she asked.

"Exactly what you planned to do. Go back to Oklahoma, go to OU, and enroll in law school." He paused. "Then we'll see what happens."

The papers around the country carried the news of Ada's victory. Most of them praised the Supreme Court for being so decisive and quick. Oklahoma's Chancellor of Higher Education said the state would comply with the Supreme Court's decision. The story Ada liked best was one in the Oklahoma City paper that showed that 82% of all OU law students looked forward to welcoming Ada into their classes.

Ada knew that no matter how positive most people were, there would also be some who opposed her. But what did it matter now? The Supreme Court said she could go to law school!

When Ada's airplane arrived back in Oklahoma, a huge crowd met her. People cheered her when she stepped off the plane. Her mother ran up and gave her a hug. Several others brought her flowers. Newspaper reporters from all over the country greeted her, too.

"Mrs. Fisher," one of them asked, "how did you get the courage to fight this battle for so long?"

She smiled. "My late father always told me that anything worth having was worth fighting for. And this was definitely worth having."

"Did you ever think you would win this fight?"

"I always thought I would win," she answered, grinning. Then she added in a softer voice: "I just wasn't sure how long it would take."

Another reporter jumped forward, taking down her remarks in a little notepad. "What do you think of our government now, Mrs. Fisher?"

Ada thought for a moment. "I think we have a wonderful Constitution. That's something we can all be proud about."

"Are you glad you went through all this trouble?"

Ada nodded. "As long as I can remember, I've wanted to be a lawyer. Now my dream is going to come true."

When she said it, though, Ada noticed a strange expression on Mr. Dunjee's face, then on her mother's face, too. It was obvious that they knew something she did not. Suddenly she was anxious to get away from these kind well-wishers so she could hear what had happened.

The U.S. Supreme Court had ordered the Oklahoma Supreme Court to direct the board of regents to admit Ada to law school. When the Oklahoma Court issued its order, however, it was not what Ada and her lawyers had expected. The state court noted that Oklahoma law still required segregated schools. Since the U.S. Supreme Court had not specifically said those laws were unconstitutional, they were still in effect and must be enforced. Therefore, the board of regents had two choices. It could immediately create a separate school for Ada and any other interested black students to study law. Or it could close down the existing law school for white students. Either way, the state would be providing students of both races equal opportunities—without violating the state laws requiring segregated schools.

Ada was appalled. "I don't believe it. They would close down the law school just to keep me out?" She tried not to let it hurt her feelings. But how could she help it? All she wanted was to go to law school. Most of the other students wanted her there, too.

"They won't shut down the law school," Dunjee told her. "That would upset too many mommies and daddies who vote." "Then what will they do? The Supreme Court said they had to admit me this semester. They can't create a whole new law school in five days!"

As it turned out, that was exactly what the board of regents decided to do.

The state attorney general, Mac Q. Williamson, acting in connection with Governor Roy J. Turner, ordered the board of regents to create a   Langston University College of Law. Since Langston had no facilities for a law school, the school would be located at the state capitol. The students could use the law library already there. Three rooms on the fourth floor would be turned into classrooms. One local lawyer was appointed to act as the dean. Two more lawyers were appointed to be the teachers. According to the attorney general, the school would be ready in time for the fall semester.

The state had created a law school for one student. In five days.

All the newspapers and radio programs talked about the surprising turn of events. Could a school slapped together so quickly possibly be equal to the well-established school at OU? Could a school created in five days equal a school that had existed for five decades? Most people thought it was impossible. They considered this a token effort to satisfy the Supreme Court without really changing anything. Other states took the Supreme Court's words seriously. The president of the all-white University of Arkansas announced that, based on the Sipuel decision from the Supreme Court, he would begin admitting black students. Nonetheless, in Oklahoma, the state refused to let Ada in.

As part of the state's effort to show that Langston was equal to other schools, they allocated some money for improvements. For the first time in its history, the state paved the streets at Langston University. The students were no longer washed in mud every time it rained. As a result of the improvements, Langston finally received accreditation.

The battle Ada had begun more than four years earlier to improve Langston had been advanced, if not won. But how long would it take to win this new battle? Just when her dream of attending OU law school was finally in her grasp—it was snatched away at the last possible moment. Thurgood Marshall joked and tried to keep their spirits up. But Ada could see that even he was disturbed. "I've heard of instant coffee," he said, "but I've never heard of instant college."

"So what do we do now?" Ada asked.

"The question," Dunjee said, "is what you want to do. You could enroll in this make-believe school they've created. Then after it proves to be worthless, we can go back to court and argue that you are not getting an education equal to what white students get at OU."

"No," Ada said firmly. "I didn't fight this battle for two years just to end up at some sad sack college that doesn't even have its own library!"

"We can go back to court and challenge this," Marshall said. "We can say that the state is not obeying the U.S. Supreme Court's order. We can insist that you be admitted at OU. But you know what that means."

Ada thought she did, but did not want to say it aloud.

"It means we'll have to start all over again. You'll have to go back to OU. You'll have to reapply for admission."

"And they'll turn me down again."

"That's right. And then we go to court seeking another *writ of mandamus*. But this time we'll have something we didn't have before. A written opinion from the Supreme Court. *Sipuel v. Board of Regents of the University of Oklahoma*. An order from the highest court of the land saying that this state—that all states— must provide all students an equal chance at an education."

Ada frowned. "Will it take as long this time as it did before?"

"Probably."

Dunjee stepped in beside her. "It's your decision, Ada. What do you think?"

Ada did not hesitate. "I say, my parents didn't raise any quitters. Who's going to drive me to the admissions office?"

12

SEPARATE IS NEVER EQUAL

Once again, Ada applied to the OU Law School and, just as before, her application was denied. Dr. Cross was still kind and friendly. He provided them a letter explaining that although Ada was qualified for law school, he was required by the state to turn her down because of her race. Ada's lawyers filed an action with the district court in Norman protesting her denial. Then there was nothing to do but wait for the next court date.

The sham law school at the state capitol started without Ada. At first, it had no students. Finally, after the enrollment period was extended, one black man enrolled. At the end of the semester, he had a straight-A average. Ada wondered if that was because there were three teachers for only one student. Or perhaps it was because he set the curve in every class. While Ada awaited her court date, another important development occurred. Six other black students came to Dr. Cross's office and applied for admission to six different graduate schools. They said they were applying based upon the Supreme Court's decision in the *Sipuel* case. Since there were no graduate schools for black students, OU either had to admit them or close their schools for white students. No one was sure what to do.

Ada's case was back in Norman again, but this time there would be a trial, not just a hearing. Judge Justin Hinshaw was in charge. Both parties were able to call witnesses to support their arguments. The state called several important education officials to prove that the instant law school was the equal of OU. After they testified, Thurgood Marshall cross-examined them. He could ask them any questions he wanted about their testimony.

When Thurgood Marshall cross-examined the state's witnesses, Ada saw a new side of him. He had always been so kind and friendly to her. He was not friendly, however, to the men he cross-examined. Before, he had always been courteous and respectful in court. This time, when he thought someone was lying, or saying something absurd, he did not hesitate to say so.

Ada realized that Marshall probably did not enjoy this, but it was his job. As before, they did not expect to win the trial. They were only making a record so the case could be taken back to the Supreme Court on appeal. It was important, however, that the justices be able to understand how the state of Oklahoma was trying to avoid their ruling. The justices could not conduct their own investigation. The only evidence they could review would come from the record of the trial court hearing. Therefore, Marshall tried to get everything he needed into the record.

For almost an hour, they listened to the state chancellor of education explain why the instant law school was just as good as OU's. Then it was time for Marshall to cross-examine. "How big is the library at the new college?" Marshall asked. "Well, I don't know exactly how many books they have," the chancellor replied. "But they have a lot."

"Do they have as many as the OU library does?"

"There's more to an education than having a lot of books." "But it's pretty hard to get an education without them, wouldn't you say?"

The chancellor frowned. "Our new school has books."

"Law schools in particular need books, don't they?" Marshall asked. "So the students can study previous cases." "I suppose that's true."

"And it's also true that OU has a larger library than the new school."

"They have plenty enough to—"

"In fact, isn't it true that the McAlester state prison has more books than the new school!"

"Well, I don't really—"

"How can you sit there and claim that these two schools are equal when you give more books to a prison than you give to the black college?"

The chancellor was very glad when he was finally able to step down from the witness stand.

The next witness was the dean of the new law school. Marshall grilled him about what classes they offered and what they were teaching their one student. In many cases, it was obvious that the so-called dean did not really know much about his so-called school. Ada began to suspect that they had given their one student good grades just to keep him from complaining. The longer the questioning went, the more nervous the dean became. Ada almost felt sorry for him.

"What goes on in those classes at your so-called school?" Marshall asked.

"The same things that go on in the classes at other colleges." "Well, most law schools teach by something called the Socratic method. That means the teachers pose questions and the students discuss them."

"I know very well what the Socratic method is."

"So are your students having a lot of meaningful class discussions?"

There was a little laughter from the gallery, until a glare from the judge shut it down. Everyone knew it would be impossible for the students to have class discussions—since there was only one student.

"Maybe not," the dean said, "but our student certainly gets a lot of individual attention."

"And as I recall," Marshall continued, "First-year students like to form study groups, to help them master all the new material. Are there many study groups at your college?"

"Obviously not."

"Most law schools put out a law review—a magazine the students write about legal subjects. Do you put out a law review?"

By this time, the dean looked very confused. "I'm—not sure."

"Do you put out any legal publication of any kind?"

"I'm—not sure about that, either."

Marshall looked disgusted. "Well, let me give you the answer then, sir. You don't."

The dean began to fidget. "I can have a perfectly fine law school without putting out any publications."

"That's odd." Marshall handed the dean a piece of paper. "That's your law school's office bulletin. I've drawn a circle around the part that discusses student fees. Do you see that?"

"Yes."

"You might especially notice the part where it talks about the fees students will be charged to support publications." The dean's face turned ashen white.

"Sir, could you please explain to me why you're charging fees for publications if you don't have any?"

"I—I—"

"It wouldn't be right to take money from your one poor student for publications that don't exist, would it?"

"Of course not. I don't know why this is in here."

"Well, I do." Marshall produced another piece of paper. "Isn't it because you copied everything in your student bulletin word-for-word from the OU law school bulletin!"

At this point, the dean looked physically ill. Amos Hall leaned toward Marshall and whispered, "Turn him loose, Thurgood." Marshall waved his hand dismissively at the witness, then sat down. If the dean of the law school could not adequately defend his own school, who could? It was obvious to everyone present that the new law school was not even a real school, much less the equal of the school at OU.

During the lunch break, the members of Ada's legal team, as well as the expert witnesses they had assembled to testify, congratulated Marshall on the successful cross-examinations. "Congratulations are fine," Marshall said, "but I'd rather have lunch."

Once again, no restaurant in Norman would serve them. Eventually, Marshall collected pennies from everyone and bought peanuts and drinks out of a vending machine.

After he handed out the food, Marshall gave Ada a stern look. "Ada, I'm in charge of trying this lawsuit."

"Yes, sir."

"So I'm putting you in charge of lunch. Don't let this happen again. Next time, pack some bologna sandwiches."

After the state finished putting on their case, Marshall began presenting Ada's case. He had called some of the smartest men in the country to the witness stand. They all condemned the state's attempt to create a new law school practically overnight.

Dean Earl Harrison of the University of Pennsylvania had visited the new school. He said it was not fit to even be called a law school. The dean of Harvard's law school and the dean of Columbia University's law school reached the same conclusion. Dr. Max Rudin at the university of California called the new school "a farce." He explained that a full student body was necessary because students learn by exchanging ideas.

Ada's favorite witness was a man named Henry Foster who was a professor at OU's law school. When Marshall asked him for his opinion about the new school, he practically leaped out of the witness stand.

"It's a fake!" He shouted. "It's a fraud!"

The judge banged his gavel and asked the witness to control his emotions. Later, Fred Hansen attempted to cross-examine him.

"You have quite a bit of feeling on this matter, don't you?"

"Yes, I do!" Foster said, exploding all over again. "And about the cheap political tricks of the politicians responsible for this disgraceful situation."

After that, the state's lawyers thought it would be best to just let Professor Foster step down from the stand.

Ada was elated when the trial was over. She thought her team had brilliantly proved exactly what they set out to prove. They showed that the instant law school was not equal to OU's law school. It was a joke created by a few politicians trying to sidestep the Supreme Court's order. More than ever, Ada understood how caring lawyers could improve the world. More than ever, she wanted to be a lawyer, too. She knew that Marshall had warned her they would not win in this court. But after that performance, she did not see how they could fail.

Judge Hinshaw reentered the courtroom and announced that he found that the new law school was "substantially equal" to OU's law school. Therefore, Ada's application for a writ ordering her admission to OU would be denied.

Outside the courthouse, a reporter asked Ada if she was giving up.

"Never," she said, masking her disappointment.

"Doesn't look to me like they're ever going to let you into that school."

Ada raised her head defiantly. "You just wait and see."

13

THE COST OF SEGREGATION

While Ada appealed her case to the Oklahoma Supreme Court, Thurgood Marshall filed a new case on behalf of one of the six black men who had applied to six other graduate schools at OU. His name was George McLaurin. He wanted to take graduate school classes in the education department. This created a huge problem for those politicians who were fighting for segregation. Even as poor as the new law school was, it was expensive. Now they were faced with the need to create six more graduate schools.

The board of regents estimated that it would cost at least ten million dollars to construct the facilities at Langston for those new graduate programs. It would take at least four years to build them. Even if they were able to do that, there were certain to be more applications by black students. Eventually, there would have to be a separate black program in every field that had a program for white students. Segregation was becoming impossibly expensive.

When Marshall went to court with George McLaurin, the state could not claim they had a sham alternate school to provide graduate level classes for him. A federal district court said that, based upon the Supreme Court's ruling in the *Sipuel* case, the state must either admit McLaurin or close down its school for white students. The state did not want to close down its school for white students. Therefore, thanks to Ada's legal battle, a black student would finally be attending OU—but it would not be Ada.

In the fall of 1948, George McLaurin enrolled at OU. By the end of the year, twenty other black students had enrolled. Because the state's segregation laws had not been struck down, however, the black students were kept separate from the white students. The black students were not allowed to sit with the white students. They were required to sit in an alcove in the back about the size of a closet. They had to peer through the door at an angle just to see the chalkboard.

They were also required to enter the library through a special side door. They had to sit at tables separated from the others by a heavy iron chain. An armed guard watched at all times to make sure they did not wander out of their designated areas. Later that year, Ada was surprised to receive a phone call from Thurgood Marshall.

"Guess what, Ada? We don't have to go back to the state Supreme Court after all."

Ada felt a brief moment of panic. "You mean we've already lost?"

"No, Ada. I mean we've already won. The state has decided to close their instant law school. It's too expensive. And since there are already black students at OU, it's pointless. Even the state courts have admitted that if there's no other school for black students—"

"They have to let me in the white school. Just like George McLaurin and his friends."

"That's right," Marshall said. "Just like them. With the same rules and . . . limitations."

Still, Ada had a problem enrolling at OU. The instant law school would not officially close until two weeks after the last day for enrollment at OU. She would have to wait another year before she could get in.

Fortunately, Dr. Cross intervened on Ada's behalf. Even though it contradicted district court orders and the board of regents, he ordered the dean of admissions to admit Ada on the last possible day, even though the new law school was not yet officially closed.

On June 18, 1949, Ada was finally admitted to the OU law school. It had been over three years—1,251 days—since she first applied.

A da could not help but be nervous as she approached Monnet Hall for her first day of class. Dr. Cross had done everything he could to help her, but she was starting the summer semester two weeks late. She was the only black student. In fact, she was the only female student that summer. Her classmates would be over three hundred white men. There was no chance that she would "blend in." Monnet Hall was a huge building. The students called it the "Law barn." As she walked down the corridors for the first time, she marveled at how nice everything seemed compared to the schools she had attended in the past.

Her first class was Constitutional Law. She was very excited about this. Since she had been the plaintiff in a major constitutional law case, it would be fun to formally study the subject. She entered the classroom—and gasped. The classroom had six levels of seats, like a small theater. In the furthest back row, in the furthest corner, there was a single wooden chair separated from all the others by a wooden rail. A pole was attached to the back of the chair. There was a sign at the top of the pole.

The sign said: COLORED.

Ada remembered again what Marshall had explained to her so carefully. The Supreme Court allowed her to go to law school—but it still had not eliminated segregation.

The room was already half-filled. As soon as she entered, everyone stared at her, waiting to see what would happen. Students began to whisper among themselves. She felt embarrassed, and awkward, and alone.

But not without courage. She had not fought so hard to be stopped by something like this. She raised her chin proudly, walked to the back of the classroom, and took her assigned seat.

As she waited for class to begin, Ada thought that nothing could possibly shock her more than seeing that sign.

She was wrong. A few minutes later, the door opened and her first professor entered the classroom.

And once again, Ada gasped. It was Dean Merrill—now Professor Merrill—the lawyer who had opposed her fight to enter law school! Now he was going to explain the meaning of the U.S. Constitution to her.

At first, Ada was dismayed. After she gave it some thought, though, her spirits brightened. Why should she let this intimidate her? He might have fought her all the way to the Supreme Court, but in the end—he lost.

How many law students could take Constitutional Law from a lawyer they had already beaten in a major constitutional law case?

As the summer progressed, Ada became more and more at ease with law school. Warren took a job at tinker air force base not too far from campus. He could drive her to class each day and pick her up later. She met another of her professors— Henry Foster. He was the man who had spoken with such enthusiasm in court about the fake law school. In time, she and Professor Merrill even became friendly. Although they continued to disagree on many matters regarding the Constitution, he was one of her favorite teachers.

Best of all, the other students were extremely kind to her. After her first class, Ben Blackstock's brother, Bob, and several others welcomed her. They told her how glad they were that she had been admitted. Because she was starting the semester late, some of the students loaned her their notes, so she could catch up on what she had missed.

"We just wanted you to know," Bob said, "that we're glad your fight is finally over."

"Thank you," Ada said quietly.

"That separate chair in the back," said another of the students, "was not our idea."

"I know that."

"If we could get rid of it, we would."

"The time will come," Ada said quietly. "Wait and see."

"In the meantime," Bob said, "would you join our study group? We need someone smart to cover Constitutional Law. And who could possibly know more about Constitutional Law than you? I mean, we've only read about it. You've lived it!"

Ada was moved by the kindness of so many of the people she met while she was in law school. But she never entirely lost her feeling of aloneness. The teachers and students were mostly kind, but she knew that there were still people hoping she would fail. If she did, many would say it was proof she should never have been admitted in the first place. Law school is hard for everyone, but Ada's aloneness, and the pressure she felt to succeed, made it even harder.

No matter how hard law school was, though, Ada never gave up. She never forgot her father's words. If it's worth having, it's worth fighting for.

And so she continued to fight.

Thurgood Marshall also continued to fight on behalf of George McLaurin and the other black students at OU. He argued that separating them from the other students violated the fourteenth amendment. They were not receiving the equal protection of the law, Marshall said, when they were kept separated from the other students.

On June 5, 1950, all nine members of the U.S. Supreme Court agreed with him.

The very next day, Ada left her assigned seat and moved down to the front row. And she never sat in the back again.

14

GRADUATION

Ada graduated from law school in August of 1951. Afterward, Mr. Dunjee arranged a huge celebration in Oklahoma City. All the attorneys and other helpers who had worked on her case came to see the proud result of their efforts. People sent flowers and gifts. She even received a present from Fred Hansen, the man who had represented the state in its long struggle against her.

Thurgood Marshall gave a brilliant speech. He said many wonderful things about Ada. Most of all, he talked about her courage.

"I have met many strong and good people in my time," he said. "Many have impressed me during my legal career. But I have never known anyone who impressed me more than Ada. She's a rebel—but she is always kind, courteous, and respectful of others. She's a fighter—but she would never hurt anyone. She's quiet—but that doesn't mean she doesn't have strength. And we have all seen the result, haven't we? This skinny, shy girl from a small rural town in Oklahoma has changed the face of this country. For the better."

Ada and Marshall talked about many things that night. At one point, Ada mentioned that she loved reading. Marshall said that books had always been important in his life, too. Ada told him that her favorite author was Mark Twain.

A huge grin spread across Marshall's friendly face. "Does that mean you like Mark Twain, too?" Ada asked.

Marshall laughed. "Do you know who gave me my first job when I got out of law school?"

"No."

"Warren McGuinn. A brilliant attorney. Started the first black law firm in New York. Taught me the ropes, after I got out of law school. Told me I should use my talent not just to make money, but to do some good in the world. I've always tried to remember that."

"He sounds like a very fine man," Ada said.

Marshall agreed. "Warren McGuinn was the first black man ever admitted to Yale Law School. And do you know why they let him in?"

Ada could not imagine.

"Because he had a letter of recommendation from a famous man he had met and impressed. That man also contributed money to help finance his legal education."

"Who was it?" Ada asked.

"A man named Samuel Clemens." Marshall smiled. "But he wrote under the name of Mark Twain."

Ada could not believe it.

"What goes around comes around, Ada. Twain helped Warren McGuinn, McGuinn helped me, I was able to help you. And the circle keeps going around, from you back to Twain and on and on. It never stops. Not so long as good people take the time to help one another. Not as long as people are willing to stick their necks out to make the world a better place."

Many people had paid close attention to Ada's struggle, including the parents of another young black girl named Linda Brown. Linda attended a separate but equal school in Topeka, Kansas, but she wanted to attend the much better school provided for white students. Thurgood Marshall represented her in a case that went to the U.S. Supreme Court—twice. Finally, in 1954, in Brown v. Board of Education of Topeka, Kansas, the Court abolished segregation, ending "separate but equal" for all time, and in 1955, declared that the integration of American schools must proceed with "all deliberate speed." The Court's decision was based in large part on its previous decision in the case brought by Ada Sipuel.

In 1967, Thurgood Marshall became the first black American appointed to the United States Supreme Court.

Ada worked as a lawyer for many years. She always remembered what Thurgood Marshall told her. She tried to assist people whenever she could. As a lawyer, she was able to help many people find justice, just as her lawyers had helped her. In her later life, she worked at Langston University, where she had once gone to school. She was a teacher and an administrator. So that she could teach even more students, Ada returned to OU and obtained yet another graduate degree, this time in history.

She worked hard to make Langston a better college. Through the efforts of Ada and others, Langston eventually became the equal of other colleges. It became fully accredited and white students began attending. Today, it is fully integrated and one of the finest colleges in the state.

Because of Ada's struggle, thousands of African Americans have attended and graduated from the University of Oklahoma—and many other public colleges in the southern states that once barred them. Thanks to her, they received the same education, under the same conditions, as everyone else. A prominent street in Chickasha, Oklahoma, not far from where Ada used to go to school every day, is now called Ada Sipuel Avenue. In 1991, the University of Oklahoma— the school that once refused to admit her—gave her one of their first Honorary Doctorate Degrees in Humane Letters. Another recipient of the new degree on the same day was Dr. George L. Cross. The following year, the governor of Oklahoma appointed Ada to the state board of regents—the group that had fought against her admission to law school for so long. The official ceremony was held outside Monnet Hall—the old "law barn." But this time, there was no special chair for anyone.

Warren Fisher died in 1987, and Ada passed away in 1995. Newspapers covered her death and many words were written about the significance of her life. She became an important symbol to many people. Through her, they learned that if something's worth having, it's worth fighting for.

Ada and Warren had two children, an adopted daughter named Charlene, and a son named Bruce. For many years, Bruce worked at the Oklahoma History Center where he helped prepare the first exhibit on the history of African-Americans in Oklahoma. Of course, the exhibit prominently featured his mother. Today, visitors from all around the world can go to the History Center to learn about the courage of Ada Sipuel.

NOTE FROM THE AUTHOR

This book has been written in conformity with the standards of the Childhood of Famous Americans series of biographies for young readers and is faithful in spirit to the values and experiences that influenced Ada Sipuel's life. History has been fleshed out with fictionalized details and conversations have been added to make her life come alive to the young reader, but the characters and events are all drawn from the life of Ada Sipuel.

The author wishes to thank the following sources that were invaluable in writing this book, foremost among them, *A Matter of Black and White: The Autobiography of Ada Lois Sipuel Fisher* (written with Danney Goble). Also of invaluable use were *Halls of Ivy*, a play by James Vance; *Simple Justice* by Richard Kluger; and *Blacks in White Colleges* by George L. Cross. Special thanks to James Vance for discussing the private interviews he conducted with Ada Sipuel shortly before her death.

ABOUT THE AUTHOR

WILLIAM BERNHARDT is the bestselling author of more than thirty books, including the blockbuster Ben Kincaid series of novels. In addition, Bernhardt founded the Red Sneaker Writing Center in 2005, hosting writing workshops and small-group seminars and becoming one of the most in-demand writing instructors in the nation. His programs have educated many authors now published at major New York houses. He holds a Masters Degree in English Literature and is the only writer to have received the Southern Writers Guild's Gold Medal Award, the Royden B. Davis Distinguished Author Award (University of Pennsylvania) and the H. Louise Cobb Distinguished Author Award (Oklahoma State), which is given "in recognition of an outstanding body of work that has profoundly influenced the way in which we understand ourselves and American society at large." In addition to the novels, he has written plays, including a musical (book and music), humor, nonfiction books, children's books, biography, poetry, and crossword puzzles. He is a member of the Author's Guild, PEN International and the American Academy of Poets.

www.ingramcontent.com/pod-product-compliance
Lightning Source LLC
Chambersburg PA
CBHW021203020426
42331CB00003B/186